D1179200

MRS BROOKES'

Baker's Dozen

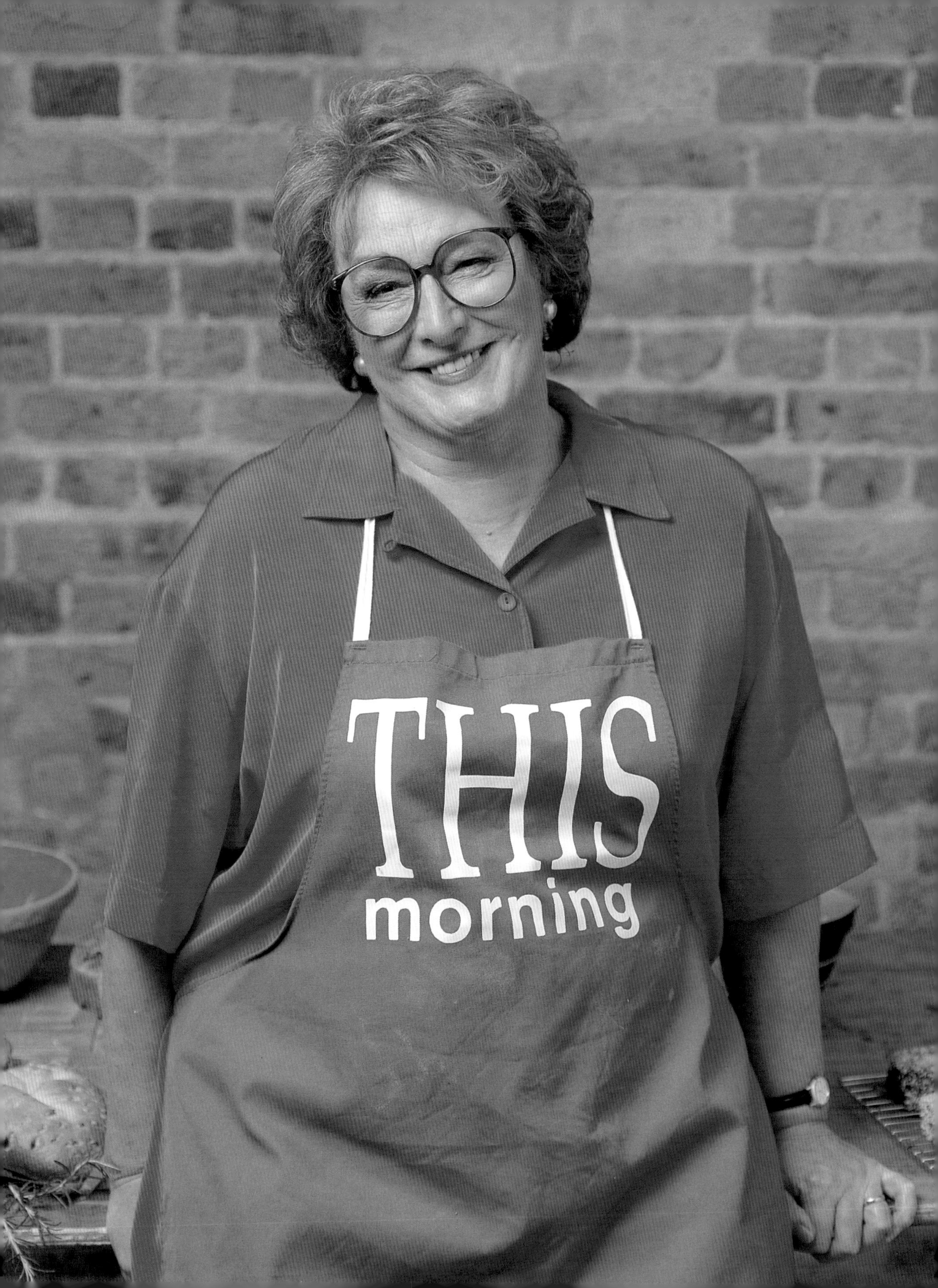
THIS
morning

MRS BROOKES'

Baker's Dozen

PERFECT HOME BAKING

GRANADA
MEDIA

For Claire Bassano
with thanks for all her help
and encouragement

For *This Morning*:
Producer/Director: Sandy Quinn
Home Economists: Claire Bassano and Yasmin Othman
Camera: Geoff Plumb and John Atkins
Sound: Brian Greene
VT Editor: Chris Clift
Managing Editor: Helen Williams
With special thanks to Warwick Hilton Brookes
for keeping the cook happy!

First published in Great Britain in 2000
By Granada Media, an imprint of
André Deutsch Limited,
in association with
Granada Media Group.
76 Dean Street
London
W1V 5HA
www.vci.co.uk

Text and photographs copyright © Granada Media Group Limited 2000
Photography by Christina Jansen

The right of Susan Brookes to be identified as the author of this work has been asserted by her
in accordance with the Copyright, Designs and Patents Act 1988.

All rights reserved. This book is sold subject to the condition that it may not be reproduced, stored in a retrieval
system or transmitted in any form or by any means, electronic, mechanical, photocopying, recording or otherwise
without the publisher's prior consent.

A catalogue record for this book is available from the British Library.

ISBN 0 233 99882 9

Book design by DW Design. www.dwdesign.co.uk

Printed by Butler & Tanner

1 3 5 7 9 10 8 6 4 2

Contents

Introduction

COOKING IS FUN – what else gives you the chance to be creative, gives everyone a treat, and allows you to enjoy it yourself as well? Indeed, when I first started writing down some of the recipes I had demonstrated on television, I can remember thinking how lucky I was that food was my area of expertise – something that most people regard with pleasure – rather than a more demanding subject such as health.

This is especially true of baking. It has been ignored a bit of late – in fact it's rather a Cinderella-stay-at-home in a world of celebrity chefs making exotic savouries to eat at the ball – but I don't think any other area of cookery can guarantee as much pleasure. Thus you will find here many favourites remembered from happy childhood times. But I have also tried to include some newer recipes that use the latest ingredients and equipment, such as blenders and processors. Something for everyone to enjoy making and tasting has been my aim.

A 'baker's dozen' is a generous sort of a measure, giving you one more than the twelve you expect, and that feeling of generosity sums up what I would like you to feel when you look at this book. If you bake, it is nearly always for others as well as yourself. If you make a cake, surely you are expecting friends to call round to eat it. Many of the recipes you will find here – both old and new – have their origin in family gatherings and in celebrations of festive events.

Lots of people who are quite confident about cooking in general are nervous when it comes to baking. This is, I think, understandable. With something such as a casserole or a curry, you can taste as you go along, and correct any mistakes in seasoning or in the thickness of the sauce in a way that you can't for a cake. With baking, you have to have the mixture right before it goes into the oven. Until you are experienced, it's important to follow a recipe rather than your instinct in order to achieve a successful result. It's also necessary to weigh and measure more carefully, and to use the right size equipment, since a mixture that will cook through and rise evenly in one size of tin may not do so in another.

I tend to use large eggs, but have said when another size is better in the recipes. A spoonful, even with dry ingredients, is always level unless it says otherwise. By all means use a processor to help with blending and rubbing in, but beware of using it all the time and of over-processing – better to give a quick burst and look, then do a bit more. The metal blade in a processor isn't good for creaming together butter and sugar, which responds better to the warmth of a wooden spoon, or your hand, and will give a lighter result. I like to do this by hand, as it is easier to see that you are getting the softness and pale colour that you want. I tend to use non-stick baking paper, which means that you don't need to grease trays and tins. The re-usable plastic fabric which you just wipe after using, though expensive, is a good investment. However, in case you don't have these, I have indicated in the recipes where you need to grease or oil trays and tins.

Nevertheless, there will be many occasions where you will need to use your own judgement and common sense. Ingredients are not always exactly the same, for example different types of flour absorb different amounts of liquid. There is also the minefield of oven temperatures – yours very probably differs a lot from mine. You should, however, be aware, unless you are using it for

the first time, whether your oven is generally fast or slow, hotter or cooler than the average. Adjust not only the temperature setting a little if this is so, but also watch your cooking times, checking a little bit earlier or later, as appropriate.

You may not be able to find the time, or have the ingredients, to rustle up all of the recipes here on an everyday basis. Most people lead busy lives, more women work outside the home than was the case in the past, and our lifestyles are very different from those of our grandmothers. Yet remember how you liked to play with a bit of pastry when you were being looked after by granny? Remember coming home to the smell of something fresh out of the oven? Remember slicing an apple pie into wedges and handing it round? If we were never to see, taste and smell these again, something precious would be lost.

So, if it's a wet Saturday afternoon, and you don't feel you want to queue in the traffic for whatever attraction is this week's favourite, think about doing things differently, stepping back a little and spending perhaps a bit less money and a bit more time. The ingredients here are for the most part cheap and readily available. The time is yours to use as you choose. The memories, with the fun, the failures and the triumphs, will be there for you to recall. But don't expect to be the greatest from your first attempt – remember how much practice grandma must have had on her mince pies.

Do please enjoy the doing as much as the eating. It's rather like Christmas, at least half the fun is in the anticipation and preparation. To bake something for friends or family to taste and enjoy is one of the very greatest pleasures, so savour it.

1 PERFECT BREAD MADE EASY

They say there's no better way to ensure a quick sale than to have the aroma of newly baked bread in the house when people are looking round – so the smell must conjure up some very positive memories!

If you have never tried to make bread before, or have tried and not done very well, please don't be put off by the thought that there is some great mystery involved; there isn't. If you follow two simple rules, I guarantee you will get that satisfying smell and taste. First, always use 'strong' flour, sold especially for bread, as it has the higher gluten content necessary for success with yeast cooking. Second, don't allow the dough to get cold. Bread likes warmth, especially during the period when you leave it to rise, and the warmer it is, the quicker the bread will rise. If you don't have a warm, draught-free place in your kitchen, look around the house; you may find somewhere unexpectedly suitable, such as a shelf over a radiator or an airing cupboard.

Take your time over the various stages and don't rush them. It will take several minutes to knead the dough to the right degree of 'elasticity' – the stage where the dough behaves a bit like rubber, and springs back when you stretch it. If your arms get tired, think of the good, cheap exercise you are getting, or invest in a machine with a dough hook. Don't be afraid to add a little more flour, or a little more liquid, if the dough doesn't feel right. Correctly mixed dough is pleasant, warm and soft to handle. If it's too dry, it may feel a bit hard and unyielding; if it's too wet, it's sloppy and sticks to your hands.

Finally, a word of warning – your bread will be so deliciously fresh, it will disappear very quickly!

White Tin Loaf

Makes 2 x 450 g/1 lb loaves

1 tablespoon dried yeast
2 tablespoons sugar
50 ml/2 fl oz warm water
25 g/1 oz butter, melted
2 teaspoons salt
450 ml/16 fl oz warm milk
850 g/1 lb 14 oz strong plain flour

1. Measure the yeast and 1 tablespoon of sugar into a jug and pour over the warm water. Leave to stand for approximately 15 minutes until the mixture becomes frothy.

2. In a large bowl mix the remaining sugar, the melted butter and salt with the warm milk and add the yeast mixture.

3. Gradually sift in the flour, mixing it in until you have a stiff dough. Alternatively, use a processor fitted with the metal blade.

4. Turn out the dough on to a floured surface and knead until smooth and elastic. Place in a bowl, cover with a damp tea towel, and leave to rise in a warm place until doubled in size (approximately 2–3 hours).

5. 'Knock back' the dough by kneading lightly for a few seconds – this expels most of the air and redistributes it evenly throughout the dough. Divide the dough into two, knead very lightly and place in 450 g/1 lb greased loaf tins or mould into shapes and place on a greased baking tray. Cover and leave to rise for a further 45 minutes.

6. Bake in an oven preheated to 200°C/400°F/Gas 6 for 40–45 minutes until golden brown and firm.

Soda Bread with Herbs

Makes 8 wedges

This bread is made without any yeast, and is a good one to start with if you are a beginner. It is best eaten fresh.

140 g/5 oz wholemeal self-raising flour
140 g/5 oz white self-raising flour
1 level teaspoon baking powder
a pinch of salt
55 g/2 oz butter or margarine, cut into pieces
2 tablespoons chopped fresh herbs, such as chives and parsley
150 ml/5 fl oz milk
a little hand-hot warm water
a little extra milk, to glaze

1. Preheat the oven to 200°C/400°F/Gas 6.

2. Put the flour, baking powder and salt into a warm bowl, and rub in the butter or margarine with your fingertips until the mixture resembles fine breadcrumbs, then stir in the chopped herbs.

3. Make a well in the centre of the flour mixture, and add the milk and just enough warm water as is necessary to bind it into a soft dough – a tablespoon at first, more if it seems stiff.

4. Turn out the dough on to a floured surface, and knead lightly until smooth. Shape into a round roughly 5 cm/2 in thick, and place on a greased baking tray. Using a knife, cut across the dough, dividing it into eight wedges, then brush with a little milk to glaze.

5. Bake for 30 minutes, until lightly browned and cooked through.

Sesame rolls (p14) and soda bread with herbs

Wholemeal Plait

Makes 1 medium loaf

450 g/1 lb strong wholemeal flour
½ teaspoon salt
1 sachet (6 g) easy blend dried yeast
1 tablespoon soft brown sugar
1 tablespoon vegetable oil
300 ml/½ pint warm water
a little milk or beaten egg, to glaze
a few sesame seeds

1. Measure the flour, salt and yeast into a large, warm bowl and make a well in the centre.

2. In a separate bowl, mix the sugar and oil with the warm water until the sugar has dissolved. Pour this liquid into the well of dry ingredients and mix together until it forms a ball of dough which comes away clean from the sides of the bowl – you may need to add a little more warm water.

3. Turn out on to a floured surface and knead until the dough is smooth and elastic – it should push out a hole made with your finger.

4. Shape the dough into a long oval and make two cuts to form three joined strands, then roll these with your hands, like working plasticine, until they are long enough to plait loosely together. Squash the ends together and tuck under.

5. Place on an oiled baking tray, loosely covered with a tea towel, and leave to rise in a warm place until doubled in size.

6. Brush the top with a little milk or beaten egg and scatter with some sesame seeds. Bake for 25–30 minutes in an oven preheated to 220°C/425°F/Gas 7, until the plait is golden brown and sounds hollow when tapped on the bottom. Cool on a wire rack.

Cornbread

Makes 1 small loaf

This is the speciality bread of the Southern states of America, where it is always served when there are red beans on the menu – they go particularly well together. In America, there are many packet mixes available, but it isn't difficult – and it's much nicer – to make your own. Try a health food store if you can't obtain coarse yellow cornmeal at the supermarket.

225 g/8 oz coarse yellow cornmeal
60 g/2¼ oz plain flour
2 level teaspoons baking powder
1 level teaspoon salt
2 level teaspoons white sugar
1 medium onion, peeled and grated
1 tablespoon olive oil
1 large egg
375 ml/13 fl oz milk

1. Preheat the oven to 220°C/425°F/Gas 7.

2. Sift the dry ingredients into a large bowl, then mix in the grated onion.

3. In another bowl, whisk together the oil, egg and milk. Make a well in the centre of the dry ingredients, pour in the egg mixture and combine.

4. Spoon into a 450g/1 lb greased loaf tin, then bake for about 20 minutes until golden brown. Allow to cool for 5 minutes before turning out.

NOTE *Sometimes a sort of skillet, or handle-less frying pan, is used instead of a loaf tin, which, because it is shallower, means the cornbread does not take quite so long to cook. Test for doneness by inserting a skewer into the centre. If it comes out clean, the cornbread is ready.*

Sesame Rolls

Makes 12 rolls

450 g/1 lb strong plain flour
115 g/4 oz fine semolina
1 teaspoon salt
2 teaspoons caster sugar
1 sachet (6 g) easy blend dried yeast
25 g/1 oz butter
300 ml/½ pint hot water
a little milk
85 g/3 oz sesame seeds

1. Measure the flour, semolina, salt, sugar and yeast into a large bowl and mix.

2. Put the butter into a jug containing the hot water, and stir together until the butter has melted. Make a well in the centre of the dry ingredients, and pour in the water and melted butter. Mix together with a wooden spoon until it forms a soft dough.

3. Turn out the dough on to a floured surface, and knead until it is smooth and elastic, about 5 minutes. Put back into the bowl, cover with a clean tea towel, and leave in a warm place for about 1 hour or until doubled in size.

4. Briefly knead the dough again, but only lightly, to evenly distribute any air holes, then divide it into twelve and shape into oval buns. Place the rolls on a large, well oiled baking tray (or use two, or a roasting tin, if you haven't one big enough) and leave, covered, in a warm place to rise again for 30 minutes.

5. Before baking, brush each roll with a little milk, and scatter the sesame seeds on top.

6. Bake for 10 minutes in an oven preheated to 220°C/425°F/Gas 7, then turn down the oven to 160°C/325°F/Gas 3 and cook for a further 15 minutes until golden brown and cooked through – a tap on the bottom should sound hollow. Cool on a wire rack.

Yorkshire Feta and Pumpkin Bread

Makes 1 small loaf

This is an adaptation of a Delia Smith recipe. It is very quick and easy to make,
and is particularly delicious in a packed lunch or with soup.

175 g/6 oz self-raising flour
1 teaspoon salt
2 pinches cayenne pepper
175 g/6 oz pumpkin, grated
½ red onion, peeled and chopped
2 rounded teaspoons chopped rosemary
115 g/4 oz feta cheese, cut into 1 cm/½ inch cubes
1 large egg
2 tablespoons milk
1 heaped teaspoon grain mustard

1. Preheat the oven to 190°C/375°F/Gas 5.

2. Sift the flour, salt and cayenne pepper into a large mixing bowl.

3. Add the pumpkin, half the red onion, half the rosemary and two-thirds of the cheese, and mix together.

4. In another bowl, beat the egg, milk and mustard together, then pour this on to the flour mixture and bring together into a dough.

5. Transfer to a greased baking tray and pat out into a circle about 15 cm/6 in across. Scatter the rest of the cheese, rosemary and onion over the surface, pressing them down a little into the dough.

6. Bake for 45 minutes or until golden brown. Allow to cool a little on a rack, and serve warm.

NOTE *The bread can be reheated in the oven the next day.*

2 | FANCY BREAD

I couldn't begin to count the number of different varieties of bread there are, and everyone has their favourites. When you travel, it is interesting to seek out the local bakeries and sample the specialities of the region, with the additional benefit that, if you try them with the local delicatessen foods for a picnic, it costs a lot less than a restaurant meal. In fact, some of the ideas I have included here are based on breads I have eaten while on holiday, in particular the Mediterranean dough that uses olive oil, and it is nice to think that something so delicious and wholesome is also good for you.

Not that I've neglected our own specialities. It is noticeable that there are many more sorts of bread for sale in the average supermarket than there used to be. This is good in many ways, but I find it a pity that in my own local shops in Yorkshire I can buy pitta and naan bread, but not the traditional haverbread or floppy oatcake that used to be the staple diet of the area. So here I have also included some old favourites alongside the new stars of the bread shop.

Stromboli

Makes 1 medium loaf

This strongly flavoured Italian bread is ideal for a picnic, being almost a meal in itself.
If you can't find provolone, use a smooth cheese such as Gouda or Edam.

450 g/1 lb strong white flour
1 sachet (6 g) easy blend dried yeast
1 teaspoon salt
3 tablespoons olive oil, plus a little extra for greasing
350 ml/12 fl oz hand-hot water

For the filling
2 balls (280 g/10 oz) mozzarella cheese
115 g/4 oz provolone cheese
85 g/3 oz prosciutto
2 handfuls basil leaves
2 tablespoons olive oil, plus a little extra for drizzling
some sprigs of thyme
coarse sea salt

1. Measure the flour, yeast and salt into a large bowl. Mix together, make a well in the centre and then pour in the 3 tablespoons of olive oil.

2. Mixing with a wooden spoon, gradually add the hot water into the well, drawing in the flour until you have a soft dough.

3. Turn out the dough on to a lightly floured surface and knead for 10 minutes, until smooth and small air bubbles appear on the surface when you wrinkle it up.

4. Wash the bowl and grease it with a little oil. Put the dough back in, cover with a clean tea towel, and leave to rise in a warm place for about 1 hour, or until doubled in size.

5. Turn out the dough again and spread it on a floured surface. Tuck the edges under to add more air, lightly knead, and repeat four times – don't over-knead as it is important not to lose the air at this stage. Cover and leave for 5 minutes or so while you prepare the filling.

6. Slice the mozzarella, cube the provolone, snip the prosciutto into bite-sized pieces, and tear the basil leaves if they are large.

7. Roll out the dough to make a 30 x 36 cm/ 12 x 14 in rectangle, and sprinkle with the mozzarella and basil. Spread over a tablespoon of olive oil, then sprinkle the provolone and prosciutto over the top.

8. Roll up the dough over the filling, as you would a Swiss roll, tucking the ends under to neaten, and place on a greased baking tray. Cover and leave for 10 minutes – it will rise only a little more at this stage – while you preheat the oven to 200°C/400°F/Gas 6.

9. Pierce the dough all over, through to the baking tray, with a two-pronged meat fork or a skewer. Tuck sprigs of thyme into most of these holes, leaving them just poking out. Brush the surface with the remaining tablespoon of olive oil and sprinkle over the coarse sea salt. Bake for 30 minutes, or until golden brown and cooked through. Cool on a wire rack. Delicious served warm.

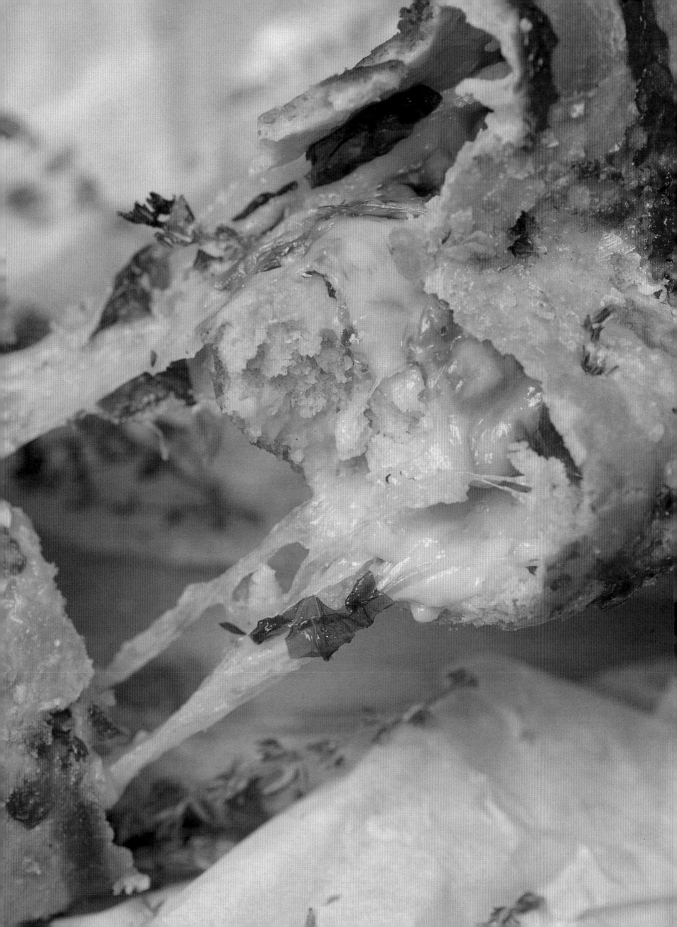

Mediterranean Plait

Makes 1 large loaf

As the dough is divided into three, you can use a variety of flavourings – black or green olives or sun-dried tomatoes, for example – or you can have them all the same, if that is what you prefer.

450 g/1 lb strong white flour
225 g/8 oz strong wholemeal flour
½ teaspoon salt
1½ sachets (9 g) easy blend dried yeast
1 tablespoon olive oil
450 ml/16 fl oz warm water

Flavourings
55 g/2 oz black olives, pitted and chopped
55 g/2 oz sun-dried tomatoes,
cut into pieces
55 g/2 oz green olives, pitted and chopped
a little oil or beaten egg, to glaze

1. Measure the flours, salt and yeast into a large, warm bowl. Make a well in the centre, and pour in the olive oil and warm water. Mix well, to form a dough that comes away clean from the sides of the bowl. You may need to add a little more warm water if it is too stiff, a little more flour if it is too sticky.

2. Turn out the dough on to a floured surface and knead for 10 minutes until the dough is smooth and elastic – it should push back out any hole you make with your finger. If you have a machine with a dough hook, it will only take 5 minutes or less to reach this stage.

3. Put the dough back in the bowl, cover with a damp tea towel or cling film, and leave to rise in a warm place for 1 hour, or until doubled in size.

4. Divide the dough into three, and flatten out with your hand to make a shape just bit bigger than your hand. Add the desired flavourings to each third, then fold the dough over the fillings and roll the pieces of dough to form long thin sausage shapes. Loosely plait the three strands together, tucking the ends under.

5. Place on a greased baking tray, cover loosely, and leave to rise in a warm place for 15 minutes.

6. Brush the top with a little oil or beaten egg to glaze and give a crisp crust, then bake in an oven preheated to 220°C/425°F/Gas 7 for 30 minutes until the plait is golden brown and sounds hollow when tapped on the bottom. Cool on a wire rack.

Small Foccacia

Makes 6 rolls

350 g/12 oz strong white flour
½ teaspoon salt
1 sachet (6 g) easy blend dried yeast
225 ml/8 fl oz warm water
1½ tablespoons fruity olive oil

For the topping
poppy seeds, sesame seeds,
coarse sea salt, sunflower seeds

1. Measure the flour, salt and yeast into a warm bowl and mix together.

2. Make a well in the centre, pour in the warm water and olive oil, and mix together to make a soft dough that comes away clean from the sides of the bowl. If you have a machine with a dough hook, process for 5 minutes, otherwise knead on a floured surface for about 10 minutes, until the dough feels elastic and pushes out the mark of a finger poked into it.

3. Put the dough back in the bowl and cover with a damp tea towel or cling film and leave to rise in a warm place for 1 hour or until doubled in size.

4. Turn the dough out on to a floured surface again. 'Knock back' by kneading gently for a minute or so, then shape the dough into six equal sized pieces. Roll each one into a ball and flatten with your hands.

5. Space the rolls out on a large, lightly greased baking tray and sprinkle your chosen topping over each one – if it doesn't stick, first brush the top with a little olive oil. Cover again and leave to rise in a warm place for a further 30 minutes – the dough won't rise as much this time.

6. Bake in an oven preheated to 200ºC/400ºF/Gas 6 for about 15 minutes – the rolls should sound hollow when tapped on the bottom if done. Allow to cool slightly on a rack and serve warm.

Christmas Stollen

Serves 8 to 10

This German speciality is made from a rich yeasty dough surrounding a marzipan middle. I'm told that it is supposed to represent the Christ Child wrapped in swaddling clothes.

450 g/1 lb strong plain flour
½ teaspoon salt
1 sachet (6 g) easy blend dried yeast
55 g/2 oz caster sugar
1 teaspoon ground nutmeg
225 g/8 oz sultanas
55 g/2 oz candied peel
100 g /3½ oz chopped hazelnuts
4 tablespoons brandy or sherry

250 ml/9 fl oz warm milk
1 large egg, beaten
175 g/6 oz butter, softened and
cut into pieces
175 g/6 oz marzipan

To finish
25 g/1 oz butter, melted
icing sugar, sifted

1. Measure the flour, salt, yeast, caster sugar, nutmeg, sultanas, candied peel and hazelnuts into a large bowl and mix together well.

2. Add the brandy or sherry, the warm milk, the beaten egg and the butter, and mix into a dough with a wooden spoon. If the dough seems very sticky, add a little more flour.

3. Turn out on to a floured board and knead for 5 minutes until elastic, then roll the dough into a rectangle about 25 x 20 cm/10 x 8 in.

4. Roll out the marzipan to a smaller rectangle, about 25 x 12 cm/10 x 4¾ in. Place on top of the dough, and pull the long sides of the dough together to cover the marzipan in the centre. Roll this parcel over so the join is at the bottom.

5. Place on a greased baking tray, cover with oiled cling film and leave to rise in a warm place for about 1 hour, or until doubled in size.

6. Remove the cling film and bake in an oven preheated to 200°C/400°F/Gas 6 for 40 minutes until well risen and golden brown. Allow to cool on a wire rack for about 10 minutes before brushing with melted butter and dusting with icing sugar.

NOTE *The stollen can be stored in an airtight tin for a week, possibly more. It also freezes well.*

Lincolnshire Plum Bread

Makes 4 x 450 g/1 lb loaves

25 g/1 oz fresh yeast
1 teaspoon sugar
2 tablespoons warm water
225 g/8 oz fat, lard or margarine, or a mixture
900 g/2 lb plain flour
350 g/12 oz caster sugar
½ teaspoon mixed spice
1 teaspoon salt
675 g/1½ lb mixed dried fruit
115 g/4 oz mixed peel
2 large eggs, beaten
a little warm milk

1. Mix the yeast with the sugar and warm water in a bowl and leave to froth for 10 minutes.

2. In a large bowl, rub the fat into the flour until it resembles breadcrumbs, then add the caster sugar, spice and salt. Mix in the dried fruit and peel.

3. Make a well in the centre, add the frothed yeast mixture, and then the beaten egg and just enough warm milk to form a soft dough.

4. Turn out the dough on to a lightly floured surface and knead until it feels elastic and pushes out the mark of a finger poked into it. Return to the bowl, cover with a damp tea towel and leave to rise in a warm place for about 2 hours, or until doubled in size.

5. Grease four 450 g/1 lb loaf tins. Divide the dough into four and press into the tins. Leave to rise again for 30 minutes, then bake in an oven preheated to 200°C/400°F/Gas 6 for 1 hour. Cool in the tin for a couple of minutes before turning out on to a wire rack to cool fully.

Brioche

Makes 1 large or 6–8 small brioche

*If you don't have a fluted round brioche mould (the one I use holds 1.5 litres/2½ pints water)
you could use a 20 cm/8 in round cake tin. The mixture will also make six to eight individual, little
brioches, in small moulds or muffin tins. These will only take 15 minutes to bake.*

**275 g/10 oz strong plain flour
1 sachet (6 g) easy blend dried yeast
2 rounded teaspoons caster sugar
½ teaspoon salt
55 g/2 oz butter
2 tablespoons warm water
3 large eggs**

1. Measure the flour, yeast, sugar and salt into a large bowl and make a well in the centre. Melt the butter in a small pan with the water. Whisk the eggs together, and put aside about a tablespoon to use for glazing later.

2. Pour the melted butter, water and the beaten egg into the flour mixture and mix to form a soft dough.

3. Turn the dough out on to a floured surface. Dust your hands well with flour, and knead for 5 minutes or so until the dough is smooth and elastic – you may have a machine with a dough hook which will do this more quickly.

4. Place the dough in a lightly oiled or buttered clean bowl and cover with a tea towel. Leave to rise in a warm place for about 1 hour until at least doubled, probably trebled, in size.

5. Turn the dough out on to a floured surface again and 'knock back' by kneading lightly for a few seconds – this expels a lot of the air and redistributes it evenly throughout the dough. Place in an oiled mould or tin, cover loosely and leave to rise for a further 45 minutes.

6. Brush the top of the dough with the reserved beaten egg and bake in an oven preheated to 230°C/450°F/Gas 8 for 20 minutes. Allow to cool in the tin for a few minutes before turning out on to a wire rack. Delicious served warm for breakfast.

NOTE *Any leftovers can be toasted or frozen.*

3 | AMERICAN-STYLE MUFFINS

If you want a round, flat-topped sort of teacake, the type of old English muffin that you would probably split and toast, then you'll have to look elsewhere. This chapter features the big buns popularized in America – isn't everything bigger over there?

If I was asked what the difference is between a bun and a muffin, I'd have to say it isn't just a question of size. Muffins should have a very full, top-heavy shape, like that of a button mushroom in cross section, having oozed and risen over the sides of their paper cases. And they are nearly always served still in their cases, as this means that they have cooled in them after coming out of the oven, and thus have kept more moist. The secret of getting that very full, top-heavy shape is quite simple – make sure you fill the cases generously, so that the mixture comes well over halfway up the sides.

There are recipes for some very indulgent muffins here – just the job, I find, for bridging the gap between getting home hungry from school and the evening meal, which, in my experience with teenagers, is the hardest one to fill. But traditionally, American muffins have some very healthy ingredients, too, such as grated carrot and all sorts of fruits and nuts – a good way of slipping a bit of variety into the family diet without them noticing.

Carrot and orange muffins (p28)
and blueberry muffins (p29)

Carrot and Orange Muffins

Makes 10

225 g/8 oz caster sugar
225 ml/8 fl oz sunflower oil
3 large eggs
200 g/7 oz self-raising flour
½ teaspoon baking powder
1 teaspoon ground cinnamon
½ teaspoon salt
225 g/8 oz carrots, peeled and finely grated
85 g/3 oz sultanas

1 tablespoon orange juice
finely grated zest of ½ orange

For the frosting
zest of ½ an orange
1 tablespoon orange juice
250 g/9 oz mascarpone cheese
2 teaspoons caster sugar

1. Preheat the oven to 180°C/350°F/Gas 4.

2. Put the sugar and oil in a large bowl, and beat together with a wooden spoon. Add the eggs one at a time, and beat in thoroughly.

3. In another bowl, sift together the flour, baking powder, cinnamon and salt, then add this, a few spoonsful at a time, to the egg and oil mixture, beating in each addition thoroughly. Then add the grated carrot, the sultanas and the orange juice and zest.

4. Line a deep muffin tray with paper cases and spoon in the mixture so that it comes fairly near to the top of each case; you want the muffins to rise above the cases, which they won't if they have been only half-filled.

5. Bake for about 20 minutes, until the muffins are well risen and springy to the touch. Cool on a wire rack.

6. Mix the frosting ingredients together in a bowl and spoon a little on top of each muffin. If you have any extra oranges, a little finely grated zest sprinkled over the top looks good.

Blueberry Muffins

Makes 6

275 g/10 oz self-raising flour
½ teaspoon baking powder
115 g/4 oz caster sugar
½ teaspoon salt
175 g/6 oz butter, cut into pieces
1 large egg
100 ml/3½ fl oz milk
½ teaspoon vanilla extract
115 g/4 oz fresh or frozen blueberries

1. Preheat the oven to 200°C/400°F/Gas 6.

2. In a large bowl, mix together the flour, baking powder, sugar and salt. Rub in the butter with your fingertips until the mixture resembles fine breadcrumbs – or use a processor.

3. In another bowl, beat together the egg, milk and vanilla extract, then pour this into the flour mixture and stir it in until all the flour is moistened – it will look a little lumpy at this stage. Fold in the blueberries.

4. Line a deep muffin tray with paper cases and spoon in the mixture so that it comes fairly near to the top of each case – you want the muffins to rise above the cases, which they won't if they have been only half-filled.

5. Bake for about 20 minutes, or until risen and golden and a skewer comes out clean from the centre. Cool on a wire rack, or eat warm.

Banana Bran Muffins

Makes about 10

275 g/10 oz wholemeal self-raising flour
150 g/5 oz soft dark brown sugar
55 g/2 oz low-fat powdered milk
25 g/1 oz oat bran
85 g/3 oz raisins
55 g/2 oz ready-to-eat dried apricots, chopped
115 g/4 oz mixed nuts, chopped
2 bananas, peeled
75 ml/3 fl oz sunflower oil
200 ml/7 fl oz orange juice
3 large eggs
a few seeds or chopped mixed nuts,
to sprinkle on top

1. Preheat the oven to 200°C/400°F/Gas 6.

2. Place all the dry ingredients – the flour, sugar, powdered milk, oat bran, raisins, apricots and nuts – in a large bowl and mix together.

3. Put the bananas into a processor or blender. Add the oil, orange juice and eggs, and blend until smooth. Mix this into the dry ingredients.

4. Line a deep muffin tray with paper cases and spoon in the mixture so that it comes fairly near to the top of each case – you want the muffins to rise above the cases, which they won't if they have been only half-filled. Sprinkle some chopped seeds or nuts over the top of each muffin.

5. Bake for 20 minutes or until well risen and a skewer comes out clean from the centre. Turn out and cool on a wire rack or eat warm.

Chocolate Pumpkin Muffins

Makes about 12

225 g/8 oz self-raising flour
115 g/4 oz caster sugar
1 level teaspoon baking powder
½ teaspoon ground cinnamon
½ teaspoon salt
225 ml/8 fl oz milk
175 g/6 oz pumpkin purée (peel, deseed
and then boil, drain and mash as for potatoes)
55 g/2 oz butter, melted
1 large egg, beaten
175 g/6 oz chocolate chips

1. Preheat the oven to 200°C/400°F/Gas 6.

2. Measure the flour, sugar, baking powder, cinnamon and salt into a large bowl and make a well in the centre.

3. In another bowl, mix together the milk, pumpkin purée, melted butter and beaten egg. Pour this into the well in the flour mixture and beat together. Add 115 g/4 oz of the chocolate chips and mix together.

4. Line a muffin tray with paper cases. Spoon in the mixture, filling the cases three-quarters full. Sprinkle the remaining chocolate chips over the top of each muffin.

5. Bake for about 20 minutes, or until well risen and springy on top. Take out and cool on a wire rack, or eat warm.

Savoury Muffins

Makes 24

You can make the basic mixture, then flavour it in different ways. The amounts given here will fill about twenty-four standard muffin cases, but you could make smaller ones, in which case it will make forty-eight, and the baking time will be correspondingly shorter – 20 minutes or less.

550 g/1¼ lb self-raising flour	*Mediterranean flavouring*	*Cheese and onion flavouring*
2 teaspoons baking powder	115 g/4 oz black olives, pitted and chopped	115 g/4 oz crisp onion pieces
1 teaspoon salt	115 g/4 oz sun-dried tomatoes, cut into pieces	115 g/4 oz Cheddar, grated
2 large eggs	a handful of fresh basil, chopped	2 tablespoons chopped parsley
450 ml/¾ pint milk		
115 g/4 oz butter, melted		

1. Preheat the oven to 200°C/400°F/Gas 6.

2. Measure the flour, baking powder and salt into a large bowl and make a well in the centre.

3. In another bowl, whisk together the eggs and milk, then whisk in the melted butter. Pour into the dry ingredients and mix well to form a soft dough. Divide into two.

4. Mix the flavouring ingredients thoroughly into each half of dough.

5. Line two muffin trays with paper cases, then spoon in the two mixtures, filling the cases more than half way.

6. Bake for 30 minutes until well risen. Take out and cool on a wire rack, or eat hot.

    NOTE *These muffins are best eaten hot, but they freeze well, and can be thawed and reheated.*

PERFECT PARTY CAKES

4

You may think life has changed a lot, that how you live is very different from previous generations, yet it is usually the case that a big event or anniversary is still, as it has been for hundreds of years, marked by a special cake. Think of weddings, christenings, Christmas and birthdays – they nearly always involve a special cake.

The thought of making such a huge and special recipe yourself can be a bit daunting, particularly when you consider that others rely on professionals to do it for them. There's nothing wrong with that: you may have other priorities for the big day. But it can be a big expense, too, and investing a bit of your own time and skill is a sign that you care about more than just paying the money.

If you are nervous, let me reassure you that it probably isn't as hard as you think and you can always have a dress rehearsal before the big day. Rich fruit cakes are all the better for being made well in advance, and the flavour improves with keeping. A shorter-life cake, such as the chocolate one in this chapter, freezes well, so you can prepare that in advance, too, and just finish off the decorating nearer the time. And you don't have to be a whizz with the icing bag to achieve a professional look. Ready-to-roll icings and decorations are available in most supermarkets, and there are also specialist cake decorating shops in most towns which will give you a wealth of ideas.

Remember, you're by no means the first person to have set out to make a special cake, and you certainly won't be the last.

Basic Cake Mixture

Makes 1 x 23 cm/9 in round cake or
2 x 18–20 cm/7–8 in round cakes

This is also known as 'half-a-pound' cake, since the ingredients all weigh 225 g/8 oz, even the eggs. This is the plain version, but it is easy to vary it with different flavours, such as 2 tablespoons of very strong black coffee, 2 tablespoons of cocoa powder or 1 teaspoon of vanilla extract, so long as you don't alter the consistency of the mixture by making it either too sloppy or too dry. To make this into a moist orange or lemon cake, add the grated zest of either 1 orange or 1 lemon to the cake mixture. After it has been baked and cooled, prick with a thin skewer or thick needle and pour over the juice so that it soaks into the cake – 2 or 3 tablespoons will be enough, more would make it go soggy. You could also try adding a flavoured liqueur in the same way, if it is not intended for children.

225 g/8 oz softened butter
225 g/8 oz caster sugar
4 medium eggs
225 g/8 oz self-raising flour, sifted

1. Preheat the oven to 180°C/350°F/Gas 4.

2. Cream the butter and sugar by beating them together in a bowl until the mixture is pale and fluffy, either by hand with a wooden spoon, or using a mixer.

3. Beat the eggs together in another bowl. Add a spoonful of the flour to the creamed mixture to prevent curdling, and then add the egg and flour alternately until both have been used up. The mixture should now be of a dropping consistency, needing a slight shake for a spoonful to fall back into the bowl.

4. Spoon either into a large 23 cm/9 in cake tin and bake for about 1 hour until springy to the touch in the middle, or divide the mixture between two 18 or 20 cm/7 or 8 in sandwich tins and bake for 30 – 40 minutes.

5. Allow the cakes to cool in their tins before trying to take them out. When they are completely cold the two rounds can be sandwiched together with butter icing (see page 126) or jam.

   NOTE *If you want a cake for a special event, make the same amount of mixture as above, but first fill six bun tins or paper cases. Divide the rest of the mixture between two 18 cm/7 in sandwich tins. The buns will take about 15 minutes to cook; the sandwich tins 30–40 minutes.*

When they are completely cold, assemble the cake by sandwiching the two rounds together with butter icing (see page 126), then halve each of the buns into semi-circles and stick these around the edge of the cake top with a little more butter icing to keep them in place – you may need to overlap them slightly to make them fit. You should now have a shape like a sunflower, which can be covered with yellow fondant icing or sugarpaste (this size needs 675 g/1½ lb rolled out to a circle about 30 cm/12 in in diameter) and decorated with chocolate buttons in the centre. Alternatively, as there are twelve little half circles, decorate it as a clock, either using bought numbers or icing writing. The clock hand in the middle, made perhaps from foil, could point to the age of the birthday person.

Double Chocolate Cake

Makes 1 x 20 cm/8 in round cake

I have used both this recipe, and the one for rich fruit cake (page 40), to make a tiered cake for a wedding or celebration. You can make either of them round or square, but for celebration cakes I usually make square ones, in tins of 15 cm/6 ins, 20 cm/8 in and 25 cm/10 in. The smallest size uses slightly less cake mixture than the amount given below (what's left over can be used to make buns). The middle size – 20 cm/8 in – takes double the quantity of cake mixture, and the 25 cm/10 in size needs nearly three times the amount. Fill and ice each cake separately, and place on covered cardboard cake squares of the same size before standing them centrally on top of each other. A finish of ribbons, giving the cakes the appearance of a pile of gift parcels with a bow on top, looks good. Cover the joins between the cake layers with icing rosettes or fancy cord – available from specialist cake shops, which will also stock many other suitable, and inexpensive, items to help you decorate.

115 g/4oz dark chocolate, broken into pieces
225 g/8 oz butter, softened
225 g/8 oz caster sugar
4 large eggs
225 g/8 oz self-raising flour, sifted
1 tablespoon cocoa powder

1. Preheat the oven to 180°C/350°F/Gas 4. Melt the chocolate in a heatproof bowl placed over a pan of barely simmering water or in a microwave (see page 81). Set aside.

2. Cream the butter and sugar by beating them together in a bowl until light and fluffy. Beat the eggs together in another bowl. Add a little flour to the creamed mixture to prevent curdling, then add the egg and flour alternately until they have both been used up.

3. Add the cocoa powder and the melted chocolate. Mix well, spoon into a greased and floured 20 cm/8 in round cake tin. Bake for 1½ hours or until springy to a touch in the centre. Allow to cool in the tin, then take out carefully.

4. To finish, cut the cake in half, spread with butter icing (see page 126) flavoured with cocoa and sandwich together. Cover the top and sides with an icing made from a little butter, 115 g/4 oz melted chocolate, 2 tablespoons water, and enough icing sugar to give a soft spreading consistency. It is nice to make a double quantity and pipe rosettes round the base or over the top.

Chestnut Gateau

Serves 10

The French version of this is called vacherin, *and is usually decorated with halves of candied chestnuts –* marrons glacés *– which are wildly expensive but delicious. Buy the smaller pieces, since the larger halves are always dearer and anyway break very easily. Chestnut purée can be bought in cans, but be aware that it is sometimes sweetened, and, if it is, leave out the icing sugar.*

For the meringue	For the filling	To decorate
6 large egg whites	450 g/1 lb can unsweetened	150 ml/¼ pint double cream
375 g/12 oz caster sugar	chestnut purée	12 pieces *marrons glacés*
150 g/5 oz toasted	115 g/4 oz icing sugar	55 g/2 oz toasted hazelnuts,
hazelnuts, chopped	4 tablespoons dark rum	chopped
	300 ml/½ pint double cream	

1. Preheat the oven to 120°C/250°F/Gas ½. Whisk the egg whites in a large, grease-free bowl until soft peaks form, then gradually whisk in the sugar until they become stiff and glossy. Fold in the hazelnuts.

2. Draw four circles 23 cm/9 in in diameter on baking parchment. Divide the meringue mixture equally between them and, using a spatula or the back of a tablespoon, spread it to fit. Place on a baking sheet.

3. Bake for 2 or 3 hours, or until thoroughly crisp. Allow to cool before peeling off the parchment and keep dry.

4. About 1 hour before you want to serve the gateau, assemble the filling by beating together all the ingredients in a bowl to make a thick, smooth purée. Place one of the meringue circles on your serving dish, and spread with a quarter of the filling, then add the next meringue. Continue until you have built up all four layers.

5. To decorate, whip the cream until thick, then pipe twelve large rosettes of cream all round the top edge. Place a small piece of *marron glacé* on top of each rosette and sprinkle the hazelnuts in the centre. Cut into wedges to serve.

NOTE *If desired, the meringue can be prepared in advance up to the end of Step 3 and stored in an airtight container where it will keep for 2 to 3 weeks.*

Three-Tiered Hazelnut Meringue

Serves 10

For the meringue
6 large egg whites
350 g/12 oz caster sugar
225 g/8 oz hazelnuts, toasted and chopped

To assemble the tiers
4 x 200ml/7 fl oz cartons crème fraîche
a selection of four fruits – raspberries, strawberries,
redcurrants, cape gooseberries, blueberries all work well

1. Preheat the oven to 120°C/250°F/Gas½. Whisk the egg whites in a large, grease-free bowl until stiff, then gradually whisk in the sugar until thick and glossy. Fold in the chopped nuts.

2. Spread half the meringue on a circle of baking parchment 30 cm/12 in in diameter. Spread the rest on two smaller circles of 23 cm/9 in and 15 cm/6 in. Place on a baking tray.

3. Bake for 2 or 3 hours or until crisp through. Allow to cool before peeling off the paper, and keep dry.

4. Place the largest meringue circle on a cake stand, and spread with two of the cartons of crème fraîche. Spread with some of your chosen fruit, then add the next layers of meringue, crème fraîche and fruit, finishing with crème fraîche and fruit piled on the top and around the sides – bunches of currants look particularly good trailing over and down the sides.

NOTE *If desired, the meringue can be prepared in advance up to the end of Step 3 and stored in an airtight container where it will keep for 2 to 3 weeks.*

Rich Fruit Cake

Makes 1 x 20 cm/8 in square cake

This recipe can be used for a Christmas, wedding or celebration cake, and should be made at least a month – ideally two months – ahead of eating, as it improves with storing.

900 g/2 lb mixed dried fruit and peel
175 ml/6 fl oz brandy
4 large eggs
225 g/8 oz butter, softened
225 g/8 oz dark brown sugar
1 tablespoon black treacle
350 g/12 oz plain white flour
1 heaped teaspoon ground cinnamon
½ teaspoon salt
115 g/4 oz ground almonds
225 g/8 oz glacé cherries

1. A few hours before baking, or the previous day, soak the dried fruit in 8 tablespoons of the brandy.

2. Preheat the oven to 160°C/325°F/Gas 3.

3. Whisk the remaining brandy with the eggs in a small bowl. Cream the softened butter with the brown sugar and black treacle in your largest mixing bowl.

4. Sift together the flour, cinnamon and salt. Add a spoonful to the creamed mixture to prevent curdling, then add the egg and flour mixtures alternately until both have been used up. Stir in the ground almonds, the soaked dried fruit and cherries – it should be a stiff mixture.

5. Spoon into a greased and lined 20 cm/8 in square cake tin. Bake for 1½ hours, then turn down the oven to 150°C/300°F/Gas 2, and continue to bake for a further 2 hours, by which time a skewer inserted in the centre should come out clean.

6. Leave the cake to cool in the tin, then remove and wrap well, or store in an airtight container. For an extra-moist cake, prick with a needle or thin skewer and pour over 2 or 3 tablespoons of brandy before storing.

Christmas Cake Glaze

Sufficient for a 20–23 cm / 8–9 in round cake

If you want to avoid the last minute rush to ice your Christmas cake, this finish can be done a week or two in advance. You will need a selection of glacé fruits and shelled nuts – enough to cover the surface of the cake – and you can glaze straight on to the top of the cake, or top it with marzipan first, according to the preference of the people who will be eating it. Use roughly equal amounts of jam and liqueur. The usual jam to use is apricot but, as this often needs to have the big pieces of fruit sieved out to make it smooth, you might like to try something like redcurrant jelly, which gives a nice rosy glow. Most people use brandy as the liqueur, but an orange liqueur or an almond one also tastes good, and the alcohol helps preserve both the fruit and the cake.

2 heaped tablespoons jam
2 level tablespoons liqueur
glacé fruits
shelled nuts

1. Gently heat the jam and liqueur in a small pan, stirring from time to time, until the jam melts and is smooth.

2. Brush the glaze over the surface of the cake, and use as 'glue' to stick on pieces of fruit and nuts, either in a pattern or randomly. Brush more of the glaze over the top of the fruit and nuts – two coats will give a good shiny finish.

3. Keep the cake in an airtight container until you are ready to eat it.

Layered Christmas Cake

Makes 1 x 23 cm/9 in round cake or a 20 cm/8 in square one

For this lighter than usual Christmas cake, you make a basic mix then divide it in four and add different fruits or flavours to each quarter. I wanted to make a rich, fruity cake that didn't use the usual dried fruit, so if you're bored by currants, this one is for you. You may want to experiment with your own ideas. Marrons glacés, chopped small, would be delicious but expensive, or try using 115 g/4 oz dried cranberries or morello cherries, soaked overnight in 3 or 4 tablespoons of brandy or sherry.

For the flavours
225 g/8 oz glacé cherries
225 g/8 oz nuts (ideally hazelnuts or almonds), roughly chopped
½ teaspoon ground cinnamon
225 g/8 oz dried apricots, cut into small pieces
½ teaspoon mixed spice
225 g/8 oz glacé pineapple

For the cake mix
225 g/8 oz softened butter
225 g/8 oz soft brown sugar
275 g/10 oz plain flour
6 medium eggs
2 or 3 tablespoons brandy

1. Preheat the oven to 140°C/275°F/Gas 1.

2. Assemble your flavours in four bowls – glacé cherries in one, nuts and cinnamon mixed in another, apricots and mixed spice in a third, glacé pineapple in the fourth. Cut any large chunks smaller, using the size of the cherries as a guide, if necessary.

3. Next, make the cake mixture by creaming together the butter and sugar until soft and fluffy in a large bowl, then add a spoonful of flour to prevent the mixture curdling.

4. Whisk together the eggs and brandy in a separate bowl. Add some to the creamed mixture, mixing in well, then some more flour. Keep adding the egg and flour alternately until both are used up. You should have a fairly stiff cake mixture.

5. Divide the cake mixture between the four bowls of flavours and mix well. Grease and line a 23 cm/9 in round cake tin, or a 20 cm/8 in square one. Spread the cherry layer on the base, and smooth over. Add the nut layer and smooth, then the apricot, and finally the pineapple layer.

6. Bake for 4 hours, or until a skewer inserted in the centre comes out clean. Leave to cool before taking out of the tin. Store, well wrapped or in an airtight container until Christmas, drizzling another 2 or 3 tablespoons of brandy over the cake in the meantime if you wish.

Three Cherry Cake –
An Italian Christmas Cake

Makes 1 x 20 cm/8 in round cake

This is based on a very old recipe, made by monks near Bologna in the Middle Ages, that uses honey, nuts and fruit in a similar way. My version is a bit richer, and will be very moist if, after the cake has cooled, you prick it and pour over 2 to 3 tablespoons of liqueur – cherry brandy would be good – and let it sink in. I usually finish this with chocolate fudge icing (see p126).

85 g/3 oz dried sour cherries	3 medium eggs
150 ml/¼ pint water	400 g/14 oz self-raising flour
100 g/3 ½ oz pine nuts	1 teaspoon ground cinnamon
115 g/4 oz butter	1 tablespoon cocoa
225 g/8 oz runny honey	200 g/7 oz natural coloured glacé cherries
100 g/3½ oz dark chocolate, broken into pieces	1 x 325 g/11½ oz jar of good quality black cherry jam

1. Preheat the oven to 160°C/325°F/Gas 3, and grease and base-line a 20 cm/8 in round cake tin.

2. Put the dried cherries and the water in a small pan, and simmer together until nearly all the water has been absorbed and the cherries have softened – about 15 minutes.

3. Meanwhile, toast the pine nuts in a dry frying pan over a gentle heat, stirring constantly to prevent them burning, until lightly browned – this much improves their flavour. Spread out on a board to cool.

4. Measure the butter, honey and chocolate into a pan, and heat gently until the butter and chocolate have melted, then stir to make smooth. Whisk together the eggs in a separate bowl.

5. Measure the flour, cinnamon and cocoa into a large bowl, then add the eggs and the melted chocolate mixture and beat well.

6. Stir in the simmered cherries and their liquid, the pine nuts, the glacé cherries and the cherry jam – this will require a bit of effort, as the mixture will be quite stiff.

7. Spoon into the prepared cake tin, and bake for about 2 hours, or until a skewer inserted in the centre comes out clean. Allow to cool for a while in the tin before turning out on to a wire rack.

5 HOME-MADE BISCUITS

Read the ingredients list on the back of some packets of bought biscuits, and you'll understand why people go to the trouble of making their own. At least when you have made something yourself from the basic ingredients you have a better idea of what is in it and if it is going to be good for you.

Biscuits were the 'hard tack' that, years ago, kept armies marching and sailors voyaging when they were far from their lines of fresh supplies. This is because a crisply baked biscuit, if kept dry and in an airtight container, will last for a long time. It is also light and easy to transport. They are still a store cupboard standby for this reason. I remember a friend telling me that her mother was reluctant to call the fire brigade when their coal fire had set the chimney alight and was a danger to both themselves and to the neighbours, because she hadn't baked, and could not stand the shame of having nothing to offer the firemen with the usual cup of tea after their lives had been saved. Sanity prevailed after she sent round to her sister, who had a tin of shortbread in the cupboard.

Rosemary Biscuits

Makes either 12 small biscuits or
8–10 larger ones

These are really a form of savoury scone. This recipe makes either twelve small savoury scones,
or eight to ten larger ones, depending on the size of the cutter.

150 g/5 oz plain flour
¼ teaspoon salt
1 teaspoon baking powder
55 g/2 oz butter
1 tablespoon chopped fresh rosemary
50 ml/2 fl oz buttermilk or skimmed milk

1. Preheat the oven to 190°C/375°F/Gas 5.

2. Measure the flour, salt and baking powder into a large bowl, then rub in the butter with your fingertips or a fork until the mixture resembles breadcrumbs. Alternatively, use a processor.

3. Mix in the chopped rosemary, then add just enough buttermilk or skimmed milk to combine the mixture into a soft dough.

4. Turn the dough out on to a floured board or surface and knead lightly. Roll out the dough to a thickness of 1 cm/½ in to make a circle 18 cm/7 in in diameter. Using a small, round pastry cutter, cut out rounds and place on a greased and floured baking tray.

5. Bake for about 15 minutes, until golden brown top and bottom; larger rounds will take a little longer.

   NOTE *These are best served warm, as an accompaniment to savoury lamb dishes or seafood. For a variation, try using thyme, basil or coriander instead of rosemary.*

Lavender Biscuits

Makes 20–24 biscuits

These biscuits are soft when warm but will crisp up as they cool. They make a good accompaniment to a rich creamy dessert such as syllabub or ice cream.

225 g/8 oz unsalted or lightly salted butter, softened
115 g/4 oz caster sugar
175 g/6 oz self-raising flour
1 medium egg, beaten
1 tablespoon dried lavender flowers

1. Preheat the oven to 180°C/350°F/Gas 4.

2. Cream the butter and sugar by beating them together in a bowl until light and fluffy. Add a spoonful of flour to prevent curdling, then mix in the beaten egg.

3. Stir in the flour and lavender flowers, mixing well.

4. Drop teaspoons of the mixture, spaced well apart, on to baking trays lined with baking parchment. Bake for about 15 minutes, until the biscuits are brown round the edge and golden yellow in the centre. You will need to do this in several batches. Leave to cool slightly on the baking trays for a few minutes, before transferring with a spatula or fish slice to a rack.

Chocolate Nut Brownies

Makes 12 squares

These brownies are delicious eaten just warm from the oven. If you want to keep them, store them in an airtight container on their own, as they are moister than the usual biscuit and will make the others go soft.

350 g/12 oz plain chocolate
225 g/8 oz butter
3 large eggs
225 g/8 oz soft light brown sugar
1 teaspoon vanilla extract
85 g/3 oz self-raising flour
175 g/6 oz pecan nuts, or hazelnuts, chopped
115 g/4 oz white or milk chocolate chips

1. Preheat the oven to 190°C/375°F/Gas 5 and grease and line a 28 x 20 cm/11 x 8 in baking tin.

2. Melt the plain chocolate together with the butter in a heatproof bowl set over a pan of barely simmering water and stir until smooth (see page 81). Pour into another bowl to cool.

3. Whisk the eggs together in a large bowl. Add the sugar and vanilla extract and mix together.

4. Continue whisking as you add the cooled chocolate. Stir in the flour, and then the chopped nuts and chocolate chips.

5. Pour into the baking tin and bake for about 50 minutes until crusty on top and firm to the touch. Allow to cool in the tin, then cut into squares.

Macaroons

Makes about 16

It's nice to be able to include a biscuit recipe made without fat – but be warned, the ground almonds used to make these crisp little mouthfuls still contain the naturally occurring oil found in the whole nuts. If you make them very small, they will need half the cooking time and can be used as decoration on top of a pudding such as trifle.

1 large egg white
85 g/3 oz caster sugar
55 g/2 oz ground almonds

1. Preheat the oven to 150°C/300°F/Gas 2.

2. In a large bowl, whisk the egg white until stiff peaks form – I use a hand-held electric whisk – then gradually whisk in the sugar.

3. Fold in the ground almonds using a metal spoon.

4. Drop teaspoons of the mixture on to a large baking tray lined with baking parchment or lightly oiled foil, spaced well apart, as they will spread during cooking.

5. Bake for about 1 hour, turning them over for the last 15 minutes, until the macaroons are crisp top and bottom, but still slightly chewy in the middle. Allow to cool on a wire rack. The macaroons will keep for at least 2 weeks in an airtight container as they are rather like flavoured meringues.

Millionaire's Shortbread

Makes 12 squares

For the shortbread
175 g/6 oz self-raising flour
a pinch of salt
115 g/4 oz butter, softened
55 g/2 oz granulated sugar

For the caramel
2 tablespoons condensed milk
1 tablespoon golden syrup
55 g/2 oz butter
55 g/2 oz granulated sugar

For the topping
115 g/4 oz milk chocolate

1. Preheat the oven to 160°C/325°F/Gas 3.

2. To make the shortbread, work all ingredients together in a bowl with your hands, or use a processor fitted with the metal blade, to form a stiff paste.

3. Press into a lightly greased, shallow baking tin of about 28 x 18 cm/11 x 7 in. Smooth the top and make level, then prick all over with a fork.

4. Bake for 45 minutes, or until just turning lightly golden and crisp. Leave to cool in the tin.

5. To make the caramel, measure all the ingredients into a pan, and heat gently until the butter has melted. Then bring up to the boil, and boil for 4 minutes. Allow to cool a little, then pour over the shortbread.

6. When the caramel is set, melt the milk chocolate, either in a microwave or in a heatproof bowl set over a pan of barely simmering water (see page 81) then spread over the caramel layer. Leave to cool again and, when the chocolate is set, cut into small squares.

Big Nutty Cookies

Makes 12

85 g/3 oz butter, softened
85 g/3 oz caster sugar
55 g/2 oz plain flour
a pinch of salt
100 g/3 ½ oz chopped mixed nuts

1. Preheat the oven to 200°C/400°F/Gas 6.

2. In a large bowl, cream the butter and sugar by beating together until light and fluffy, then work in the flour and salt to make a stiff mixture.

3. Add the chopped nuts and mix well.

4. Place teaspoons of the mixture on a large baking tray lined with baking parchment, spaced well apart, as the cookies will spread considerably during cooking.

5. Bake for 6–8 minutes, until brown round the edges and golden in the centre.

6. Allow to cool before lifting off the baking tray.

Melting Moments

Makes 12

85 g/3 oz butter, softened
85 g/3 oz icing sugar
25 g/1 oz plain white flour
85 g/3 oz cornflour
whole hazelnuts or
glacé cherries, to finish

1. Preheat the oven to 160°C/325°F/Gas 3.

2. Cream together the butter and icing sugar in a large bowl until very soft and light.

3. Sift the flour and cornflour together into the mixture, and work it in with a wooden spoon.

4. Put teaspoons full of the mixture on to a lined and greased baking tray. Press a nut or glacé cherry into the middle of each biscuit.

5. Bake for 15 minutes, and leave to cool on the tray.

APPLE-PIE ORDER

6

Apple pudding, apple pie,
Did you ever tell a lie?

The old playground rhyme shows how popular, and wholesome, and how regular a part of everyday life a cooked apple recipe was and still is. It is so often teamed with pastry that I have called this chapter, which has a range of basic pastry recipes, after the master recipe for a sort of sweet and savoury apple pie that has a long history in the north of England. It was first made hundreds of years ago to welcome back the local saint to Ripon, and it is still made in his honour today.

The absolute and basic rule for pastry is that there should be half the weight of fat to flour, but there are many variations on this theme. Pastry is a way of enclosing a sweet or savoury filling in a portable case, and is also a way of sealing in the flavour. Pies were sometimes sent on long journeys across the country as a way of paying in kind, and there are still surviving memories of huge, mammoth pies made to feed whole villages, which were baked by lighting a fire underneath them.

It is strange how often people talk about the apple pies their mother used to bake, as if you can't make one until you have some grey hairs. This has to be nonsense – or is it? Cool hands are essential when rubbing in pastry, so the fat combines without melting, and some recipes recommend you cool your fingers by running your wrists under cold water before you begin. As it is now known that hands get cooler with age, maybe there is something in the old wives' tale after all.

Ripon Apple Pie

Makes one 26 x 20 cm/10¼ x 8 in pie

'Apple pie without some cheese, is like a kiss without a squeeze . . .'

For the shortcrust pastry
350 g/12 oz plain flour
a pinch of salt
175 g/6 oz hard margarine, cut into pieces

For the filling
900 g/2 lb cooking apples, peeled, cored and sliced
115 g/4 oz granulated sugar
115 g/4 oz Wensleydale cheese, grated or crumbled
a little milk
caster sugar for sprinkling

1. Make the pastry by measuring the flour and salt into a large bowl, then rub in the margarine using your fingertips until it resembles fine breadcrumbs. Lift your hands up to get as much air as possible into the mixture. Use a fork to work in just enough cold water to bind it together into a dough, then divide it in half and set aside to rest for about an hour.

2. Preheat the oven to 200°C/400F°/Gas 6. Grease a 26 x 20 cm/10¼ x 8 in baking tin. Roll out one half of the pastry on a floured surface until is about an inch wider all round than your tin. Use it to line your tin, tucking it into the corners (but not stretching it, as stretched pastry tends to shrink in the baking). Trim the edges with a knife.

3. Layer the slices of apple on the pastry base and sprinkle over the sugar. Spread the grated or crumbled cheese over this.

4. Roll out the second half of the pastry to make a lid, but before you lift it on, moisten the edges of the pie with a little milk to help give a good seal. You may find it easier to lift the pastry lid into place by first rolling it around your rolling pin, and then unrolling it into place. Seal with your fingertips, trim the edges, and make a few slits in the top with a sharp knife to allow steam to escape. Brush the top lightly with a little more milk, and sprinkle over a little caster sugar.

5. Bake for 30 minutes or until the top crust is golden brown. Delicious either hot or cold.

Tarte Tatin

Makes 1 x 23 cm/9 in tart

This version is made with a rich sweet pastry rather than the more usual puff pastry.

For the topping
55 g/2 oz butter
55 g/2 oz soft brown sugar
6 ripe eating apples

For the rich sweet pastry
175 g/6 oz butter, cut into pieces
275 g/10 oz self-raising flour
55 g/2 oz caster sugar
1 large egg

1. Preheat the oven to 200°C/400°F/Gas 6.

2. Gently heat the butter and sugar for the topping in a small pan until melted, then pour into the base of a solid 23 cm/9 in cake tin or quiche dish – don't use a loose-bottomed one, or all the juice will leak out. You could use an ovenproof non-stick frying pan.

3. Peel and core the apples and slice into crescent shapes. Arrange neatly in circles over the base of the tin.

4. Make the pastry by rubbing the butter into the flour until the mixture resembles breadcrumbs. Mix in the sugar and then add the egg to form a soft dough. Alternatively, use a processor fitted with the metal blade, adding the egg down the funnel with the motor still running – in seconds, it will form a soft ball.

5. The pastry should be soft enough for you to pat it out, with floured hands on a floured surface, into a round big enough to fit over the top of the pie. Place the pastry over the apples, tucking it in around the edges and patting it down.

6. Bake for 30 minutes or until the pastry is crisp and golden. Allow to cool for a few minutes in the tin, before easing a knife round the edges to loosen. Place a large plate upside down on top of the pie dish, and turn over both the pie and the plate, holding them firmly together. The pie dish should now lift off to show the apples on the base coated in their juices. Serve warm.

Apple and Rosemary Strudel

Serves 6–8

I have given instructions for making pastry but, if you prefer, you can use a pack of filo pastry instead.

For the pastry	*For the filling*
1 medium egg	4 eating apples, peeled and thinly sliced
150 ml/¼ pint water	1 bunch rosemary, stripped from the stem
1 teaspoon vegetable oil	and chopped
275 g /10 oz strong white bread flour	2 tablespoons breadcrumbs
55g /2 oz butter, melted	2 tablespoons brown sugar
	1 teaspoon cinnamon
	1 teaspoon freshly grated nutmeg
	3 tablespoons sultanas

1. Preheat the oven to 200°C/400°F/Gas 6.

2. If you are making your own filo pastry, in a bowl whisk together the egg, water and oil. Measure the flour into a bowl, and make a well in the centre. Gradually add the egg mix to the flour to form a dough.

3. Turn out on to a work surface and knead until the dough becomes soft and elastic. Leave to rest for 15 minutes.

4. Meanwhile, mix together the filling ingredients in a large bowl.

5. If you have made your own pastry, roll it out into a rectangle on a floured surface and then, using your hands, stretch it out as thinly as possible on a clean tea towel. If using ready-made pastry, which comes already rolled, lay a sheet on a clean tea towel.

6. Brush the pastry all over with melted butter. Sprinkle over the apple mixture and roll up, as you would a Swiss roll, using the tea towel to help you. Transfer to a greased baking tray – you could shape it into a horseshoe if you wish – and brush again with melted butter. Bake for 30 minutes until crisp and golden brown.

Small Fruit Cheesecakes

Makes 4

For the pastry
85 g/3 oz butter
175 g/6 oz plain flour
1 dessertspoon caster sugar
a pinch of salt
1 large egg yolk

For the filling
225 g/8 oz cream cheese
1 tablespoon caster sugar
juice of ½ a lemon
2 tablespoons set natural
yoghurt

For the glaze
2 tablespoons clear
(jelly) jam
1 tablespoon water

For the fruit topping
2 nectarines or peaches
12 cherries
4 strawberries

1. Preheat the oven to 200°C/400°F/Gas 6.

2. Make the pastry by rubbing the butter into the flour in a large bowl with your fingertips until the mixture resembles fine breadcrumbs. Add the sugar and salt, then bind together with the egg yolk. This should be enough to bring the pastry together, but if not, add a very little cold water.

3. Grease four small round tins or Yorkshire pudding trays – mine are about 7.5 cm/3 in in diameter. Roll out the pastry on a lightly floured surface and cut out rounds large enough to line the tins.

4. Bake 'blind' for 10 minutes. If you don't have the baking beans for this, a little crumpled foil placed inside each pastry case will help them keep their shape. Remove the foil or baking beans and return to the oven for a further 5 minutes. Allow to cool in the tins, then take out carefully.

5. Make the cheesecake filling by beating together all the ingredients in a bowl until well mixed. Spoon into the cooled pastry cases, smooth over the tops, and chill.

6. Prepare the fruit topping by halving and pitting the nectarines or peaches, and arranging one half on top of each little cheesecake, piling the other fruit around.

7. The glaze is made by melting the jam in a small pan with a spoonful of water over a gentle heat. Stir until smooth, then brush generously over the fruit topping and leave to set.

Lemon Tart

Makes 1 x 20 cm/8 in tart

For the pastry
175 g/6 oz plain flour
85 g/3 oz butter, cut into pieces
zest of ½ a lemon
1 dessertspoon caster sugar
1 large egg

For the filling
2 large eggs
55 g/2 oz caster sugar
55 g/2 oz ground almonds
zest of 1½ lemons
juice of 2 lemons
a little icing sugar, for dusting

1. Preheat the oven to 200°C/400°F/Gas 6.

2. To make the pastry, measure the flour, butter, lemon zest and sugar into a processor fitted with the metal blade. Process until the mixture resembles breadcrumbs and then, with the motor still running, pour the beaten egg down the funnel and in a few seconds the mixture will come together into a ball. Alternatively, rub in the butter with your fingertips in a bowl, using the egg to bind the dough.

3. Roll the dough out on to a floured surface and use to line a 20 cm/8 in greased pie dish. Bake 'blind', lined with foil and baking beans, in the centre of the oven for 10 minutes, then remove the foil and beans and bake for a further 5 minutes until the pastry is set. Leave to cool a little while you make the filling. Turn down the oven to 180°C/350°F/Gas 4.

4. To make the filling, whisk together the eggs and sugar in a large bowl until they have doubled in size and are thick, pale and foamy – the whisk should leave a trail when lifted. I find this easiest to do with a hand-held electric whisk. Add the ground almonds, lemon zest and juice, and mix well before pouring the filling into the pastry case.

5. Bake the tart for 30 minutes, or until the filling is just set. Allow to cool a little before dusting with icing sugar. Can be eaten either warm or cold.

Bakewell Pudding

Makes 2 x 20 cm/8 in puddings

The Derbyshire lass who gave me this recipe insists it is called pudding, though it seems to me to be a pastry based tart. It can be made using either shortcrust or puff pastry, depending on your preference, but either way you will need enough to line two 20 cm/8 in round pie dishes. As the pudding freezes well, I usually eat one fresh, then freeze the other.

shortcrust or puff pastry to line two 20 cm/8 in pie dishes, see pages 54 and 63
3 heaped tablespoons raspberry jam
225 g/8 oz butter
3 large eggs
225 g/8 oz caster sugar
115 g/4 oz ground almonds or ground hazelnuts

1. Preheat the oven to 200°C/400°F/Gas 6.

2. Line the two greased pie dishes with the pastry, divide the jam between them and spread over the bottom of each.

3. Melt the butter in a small pan, and then allow to cool a little – I find the quickest way to do this is to pour it out of the pan into a bowl.

4. In a separate bowl, beat the eggs together, then add the sugar and the melted butter and mix well. Stir in the ground nuts, then carefully pour over the jam.

5. Bake for 10 minutes, then turn down the heat to 160°C/325°F/Gas 3 and cook for a further 15 minutes or until the filling has just set. It sinks a little when it cools. Best served hot, or warm.

VARIATION *Instead of two puddings, you can make one large one in a 29 x 20 cm/11½ x 8 in baking tin. Scatter 55 g/2 oz flaked almonds over the top before baking. It will take 5 or 10 minutes longer in the oven. Then serve it sliced into squares at tea-time.*

7 | FANCY PASTRY

I heard a quote recently, that life was 'too short to make pastry'. It used to be that life was too short to stuff a mushroom, but I suppose times move on. There may be some truth in this – I admit that I usually buy filo or puff pastry – but I do think that, on occasions, it is satisfying to make your own, tailoring it to suit the filling, as in the various examples in this chapter. If nothing else, when you have had a go at it yourself, you are better able to assess the bought brands, and to understand how you can improve on them or use them to help you to take short cuts.

The interest is not only in the case and the filling, but in the different shapes that can be made with pastry. This can be a great source of fun and experiment, especially if you are baking with some children around – after all, before there was Plasticine or Playdough, children learnt how to mould shapes by being given a bit of the cook's pastry scraps.

Fruit Turnovers in Flaky Pastry

Makes about 8

For the pastry
175 g/6 oz butter
225 g/8 oz plain white flour

For the fruit filling
2 tablespoons prepared fruit – diced apple,
diced pear, a selection of fresh or frozen
summer berries – per turnover
caster sugar to taste, approx. 1
dessertspoon per turnover
a little beaten egg or milk, to glaze

1. Weigh the amount of butter you need for the pastry, and put it in the freezer for at least 30 minutes, so that it gets really firm.

2. Measure the flour into a large bowl, then take the butter out of the freezer. With your hand in an oven glove, hold it in a piece of foil or greaseproof paper – this is to keep the warmth of your hand away from the butter while you grate it; it needs to stay firm. Dip the edge of the butter into the flour and then, using the coarsest side of your grater, grate it into the flour, forking it into the flour with your other hand as you go, to coat it. Continue dipping, grating and forking – you will need to keep swapping hands, to release more butter to grate – until all the butter is grated into the flour.

3. You can now abandon both foil and oven glove, but use the fork to thoroughly mix the flour and butter, before adding just enough cold water to bring the ingredients together into a soft dough. Chill, covered, in the fridge for about 30 minutes.

4. Roll out the chilled pastry on a floured surface to a thickness of about 3 mm/⅛ in, then cut out eight rounds, using either your largest pastry cutter, or cut round the edge of a small saucer.

5. Spoon 2 tablespoons of sweetened fruit into the centre of each round, then moisten the edge of the circle of pastry with a little water, and fold over in half to enclose the filling. Press the sides of the pastry together to give a good seal – I usually do this with a fork as it makes a nice pattern around the edge.

6. Brush the top of each turnover with a little beaten egg or milk to glaze. Place on a greased baking tray and bake in an oven preheated to 200°C/400°F/Gas 6 for 20 minutes, or until crisp and brown. Remove from the baking tray with a fish slice, and allow to cool a little before eating, as the fruit will be very hot.

NOTE *Don't add salt to the pastry unless you are using unsalted butter, in which case add a good pinch.*

Apple and Marzipan Circles

You can use either the basic flaky pastry recipe given on page 63 for these, or bought puff pastry.

For each person you will need
a circle of pastry, ready rolled,
about 10 cm/4 in in diameter
a circle of marzipan rolled out to the same thickness,
but a little smaller – about 7 cm/3 in in diameter
½ an eating apple, peeled, cored and sliced into rough crescents
a little melted butter
a pinch of ground cinnamon

1. Preheat the oven to 200°C/400°F/Gas 6.

2. Place the circle of pastry on a greased baking tray, then lay the circle of marzipan on top.

3. Arrange the apple slices on top in an overlapping circle.

4. Add the ground cinnamon to the melted butter and brush this over the top of the apple slices.

5. Bake for 15 minutes, or until the pastry round the edge looks golden brown and crisp. Eat while still warm, with cream or plain yoghurt if desired.

NOTE *To avoid the pastry going soggy, heat the baking tray*
in the warmed oven before putting the circles on.

Savoury Puff Tarts

Makes 2 large rectangular tarts, 1 of each flavour, each serves 2

1 x 450 g/1 lb packet ready-rolled puff
pastry sheets
a little milk

For the tomato, avocado and Parma ham filling
1 x 200 g/7 oz tub cream cheese, or
benecol, or mascarpone
1 heaped tablespoon tomato purée
1 avocado pear, halved, pitted and sliced
3 slices Parma ham or prosciutto

For the cheese, mushroom and sesame filling
1 tablespoon olive oil
½ a large onion, or 1 small one,
peeled and chopped
1 clove garlic, peeled and crushed
55 g/2 oz mushrooms, chopped
salt and black pepper
½ a 440g/15 oz jar or can peeled red pepper,
or 1 fresh red pepper, skinned
and deseeded
115 g/4 oz mozzarella cheese, sliced
1 tablespoon sesame seeds

1. Preheat the oven to 220°C/425°F/Gas 7.

2. Place half the pastry on lightly oiled foil, or use baking parchment. Cut out a border to a width of about 25 mm/1 in all round, then brush a little milk round the edge of the rectangle left in the middle, again to a width of about 25 mm/1 inch.

3. Lift the border on top of the centre rectangle to give you a double border – as it is bigger than the centre, the border will need to have the corners folded up to fit. Prick all over the middle with a fork, to prevent the centre rising too much. Place on a baking tray. Repeat with the remaining pastry.

4. To make the tomato, avocado and Parma ham filling, mix together the cream cheese and tomato purée in a bowl – I find this easiest to do with a fork. Spread evenly over the centre of the pastry, and place the slices of avocado over the top. Bake for 15 minutes, then add the slices of ham. Return to the oven and bake for a further 5 minutes.

5. To make the cheese, mushroom and sesame filling, heat the oil in a frying pan, and cook the onion, garlic and mushrooms until soft. Spoon this mixture over the centre of the pastry rectangle, spreading it evenly, and season to taste with salt and pepper. Then add the slices of red pepper and the cheese. Bake for 15 minutes, then sprinkle the sesame seeds over the top, return to the oven and bake for a further 5 minutes.

Apricot Lattice with Cream Cheese Pastry

Makes 1 x 20 cm/8 in tart

150 g/5 oz butter, at room temperature
115 g/4 oz cream cheese, at room temperature
225 g/8 oz plain flour
3 tablespoons caster sugar
a little icing sugar for dusting, if desired

For the filling
450 g/1 lb ready-to-eat dried apricots
55 g/2 oz caster sugar
150 ml/¼ pint water
3 teaspoons arrowroot

1. Remove the butter and cream cheese from the fridge at least 30 minutes in advance. Preheat the oven to 190°C/375°F/Gas 5.

2. Place all the pastry ingredients in a large bowl and mix together with your hands – their warmth helps them to combine.

3. When you have a smooth mixture, divide it into unequal portions of a third and two-thirds, and put the smaller portion into the fridge wrapped in cling film. Use the larger portion to line a 20 cm/8 in greased pie dish, patting the pastry out with your fingers, then put this into the fridge too to firm up while you make the filling.

4. Place the apricots, sugar and water in a pan, bring up to a simmer, and cook for about 10 minutes until the apricots are soft. Remove the apricots with a slotted spoon (reserving the juice) and arrange them on the pastry base so they overlap in concentric circles.

5. In a bowl, mix the arrowroot to a smooth paste with a little water, then add this to the apricot juice. Bring to the boil, and cook until the juice thickens and goes transparent. Pour over the apricots in the pie dish.

6. Roll out the remaining pastry and use a lattice cutter if you have one to make the lid. Otherwise cut the pastry into strips about 5 mm/¼ in wide and use these to make a lattice pattern over the apricots, twisting them as you go, and fixing the ends to the edges of the pie with a dab of water.

7. Bake for 30 minutes, or until the pastry is crisp and golden. Serve warm or cold, dusted with some sieved icing sugar if desired or with a spoonful of crème fraîche.

Choux Pastry

Makes 16 to 18 little choux pastry balls

Use this basic recipe for both croque-en-bouche *and profiteroles, as described below.*

2 large eggs
70 g/2½ oz strong plain flour
1 teaspoon caster sugar
55 g/2 oz butter, cut into pieces
150 ml/¼ pint water

1. Grease or line with baking parchment a large baking tray, and then, using your fingers or a spray, sprinkle cold water over the surface – this will add steam during baking. Preheat the oven to 200°C/400°F/Gas 6.

2. Beat the eggs and, in a separate bowl, mix together the flour and sugar.

3. Gently heat the butter with the water in a small pan, stirring with a wooden spoon until the butter has melted and the liquid is just coming up to the boil.

4. Take the pan off the heat, add the flour and sugar mixture, and beat with the wooden spoon, or an electric whisk if you have one. When you have a smooth ball that comes away clean from the sides of the pan, start adding the beaten egg, a little at a time, beating well until you have a smooth, slightly shiny paste.

5. Spoon small balls of the mixture on to the baking tray – I find it easiest to do this using two teaspoons. Bear in mind that the balls will increase in size during cooking.

6. Bake for 10 minutes, then increase the heat to 220°C/425°F/Gas 7, and cook for a further 15 minutes until crisp and golden. Remove from the oven, then use a sharp knife to make a vent in the side of each one to let out the steam before cooling on a wire rack.

For profiteroles

If you are making profiteroles, the pastry buns should be filled with whipped cream, perhaps with a little brandy added, as near as possible to serving time – they will go soggy if prepared too soon. Pile them up on a serving dish, then pour over a chocolate sauce, so that it drizzles down the sides. Make the sauce from 225 g/8 oz dark chocolate, broken into pieces and melted together with a knob of butter and 2 tablespoons of brandy or orange liqueur (see page 81).

For croque-en-bouche

Make double the above quantity of the choux pastry buns and fill with a mocha cream made from 600 ml/1 pint double cream whisked together with 2 tablespoons coffee liqueur, such as Tia Maria or Baileys, until thick. To make the *croque*, or spun sugar web, you need to gently heat 150 g/5 oz granulated sugar with 150 ml/¼ pint water until the sugar crystals have melted. Bring up to the boil, and continue to boil without stirring, until you have a medium caramel. This stage will have been reached when a sugar thermometer measures 140°C/275°F, or a strand of the liquid forms a thread that snaps between two teaspoons – test by dropping a little into a cup of ice-cold water. Use the syrup to stick the filled choux buns together into a pyramid shape, drizzling over any remaining syrup. Or try spinning threads of the sugar syrup to make a 'web' over and around the piled-up buns. It will quickly set to a crunchy texture as it cools.

Eclairs

Makes about 12

choux pastry, see page 68
300 ml/½ pint double cream,
whipped until thick

For the icing
6 heaped tablespoons icing sugar
1 heaped tablespoon cocoa powder
a little cold water

1. Preheat the oven to 200°C/400°F/Gas 6.

2. Using an icing bag with a large nozzle, pipe the choux pastry into sausage shapes of about 5–7.5 cm/2–3 in long on to a greased baking tray. Alternatively, make the shapes using spoons, but, either way, remember to leave plenty of room for expansion in the oven. Bake for 20 minutes then turn the oven up to 220°C/425°F/Gas 7 for 15 to 20 minutes, until crisp and golden brown.

3. When you take the pastries out of the oven, split them lengthwise and open them out a little to cool. When the pastries are cold, fill them with the whipped cream, then fold together again.

4. Make the icing by mixing together all the ingredients in a bowl. Spread on top of each of the eclairs.

NOTE *As an alternative you can dip the eclairs into melted chocolate*

Croque-en-Bouche (p69)

Coffee Cream Puffs

Makes about 12

The method is basically the same as for eclairs, but, for some reason, coffee cream puffs are usually round, not long.

choux pastry, see page 68
300 ml/½ pint double cream, whipped until thick

For the coffee icing
2 heaped teaspoons instant coffee granules
2 tablespoons very hot water
5 tablespoons icing sugar

1. Preheat the oven to 200°C/400°F/Gas 6.

2. Using an icing bag with a large nozzle, pipe the choux pastry into twelve large balls on to a greased baking tray. Alternatively, use spoons to do this. Either way, remember to leave plenty of room for expansion in the oven. Bake for 15 minutes then turn the oven up to 220°C/ 425°F/Gas 7 for 15 to 20 minutes, until crisp and golden brown.

3. After removing the balls from the oven, carefully cut them open and pull apart slightly to allow to cool. When cold, fill with the whipped cream.

4. Make the coffee icing by dissolving the coffee granules in the very hot water. Add the icing sugar until you have a consistency just runny enough to spread on top of each choux puff.

Pinwheels

Makes about 20

1 x 375 g/12 oz packet ready-rolled puff pastry
1 x 450 g/1 lb jar mincemeat
85 g/3 oz marzipan, chilled

1. Preheat the oven to 220°C/425°F/Gas 7.

2. Lightly flour your work surface, and open out the pastry on to it. You want a rectangle of about 20 x 28 cm/11 x 8 in.

3. Spread just over half the mincemeat over the upper two-thirds of the rectangle, leaving a narrow margin of about 1.5 cm/½ in at the edge to allow you to seal the pastry.

4. Using the coarsest grade, grate just over half the chilled marzipan over the mincemeat.

5. Moisten the edge of the pastry with a little water. Fold the bottom third of the pastry over to the middle, then carefully fold over the top third to fold the rectangle in half. Press the edges firmly together with your fingertips to seal.

6. Carefully roll out the filled rectangle to double its size. Spread the upper two-thirds with the rest of the mincemeat, then grate over the rest of the marzipan.

7. Fold the pastry as before, moistening the edges first to seal. Press a little flatter with the rolling pin, then roll up like a Swiss roll from the short end. Cut this sausage shape into pinwheel rounds, and place on a greased or lined baking tray.

8. Bake for 10 minutes, then flip the pinwheels over with a fish slice and bake for a further 5 minutes on this side. Allow to cool a little on a rack, but serve warm.

STOVE-TOP BAKING | 8

One of the earliest methods of cooking was on a flat stone that had been heated in the fire. Flat iron griddles, which had a hooped handle to swing them over the kitchen fire, were developed from this. I can cook directly on the hot plate of my stove at home, just using a special, non-stick paper, which saves on the washing up. If you aren't able to do this, and don't have a griddle, you probably have a non-stick frying pan that would be suitable for the recipes in this chapter.

Getting the temperature just right is important here, and generally it needs to be a low heat, or you will find your cakes burn on the outside before they are cooked through. Always warm the pan for a minute or two before you start, that way the heat will be evenly spread over the surface.

There are lots of regional variations in the way these sort of small cakes are made, as you can tell from the names of the recipes. They are a good way to start baking, as the food isn't hidden away in the oven and the beginner can see what is happening. Like pancakes, you cook most of them in batches, one side at a time and, as with pancakes, you often find that the first one isn't so good, usually because the pan hasn't heated through. There's an old tradition round here that the first pancake is always one to throw to the hens outside the kitchen door, and the ingredients are cheap enough for that not to seem too wasteful.

Welsh Cakes

Makes about 12

These were traditionally made on a griddle, a flat, iron baking tray that fitted over the fire. Nowadays, the nearest equivalent is probably a heavy non-stick frying pan set over a gentle heat.

225 g/8 oz self-raising flour
a pinch of salt
1 teaspoon mixed spice
55 g/2 oz butter or margarine
55 g/2 oz lard, or white fat
85 g/3 oz caster sugar
85 g/3 oz currants
1 medium egg, beaten
a little milk, if necessary

1. Sift the flour, salt and spice into a mixing bowl, then rub in the fats with your fingertips until the mixture resembles fine breadcrumbs.

2. Stir in the sugar and currants. Add the beaten egg, and mix together to make a firm dough, adding a little milk if you need to, to bring it together.

3. Roll out the dough on to a floured surface to a thickness of about 5 mm/½ in. Cut into circles with a 4–5 cm/1½–2 in pastry cutter.

4. Cook on a medium hot griddle or frying pan (greased unless they are non-stick) for a few minutes on each side, until golden brown but still a little soft in the middle. Eat fresh, buttered.

Welsh cakes and crumpets (p76)

Crumpets

Makes about 8

175 g /6 oz plain flour
175 g /6 oz strong white flour
1 teaspoon salt
15 g/½ oz fresh yeast
1 teaspoon caster sugar
350 ml/12 fl oz warm milk
½ teaspoon bicarbonate of soda
3 tablespoons warm water
a little butter

1. Sift the flours and salt together into a large bowl, and make a well in the centre.

2. Dissolve the yeast and sugar in the warm milk and pour into the flour mixture. Beat together until you have a smooth batter. Cover and leave to rise in a warm place for 1 hour.

3. Mix the bicarbonate of soda with the warm water in a bowl and beat into the batter for 2–3 minutes. Cover and leave to rest for 20–25 minutes.

4. Butter the insides of some 10 cm/4 in straight-sided rings and lightly butter a griddle. Put the rings on the griddle and place over a medium heat. Using a dessertspoon, drop two spoonfuls of the crumpet mixture into each ring. Cook for 3 minutes or until you see bubbles forming on the surface. Remove the rings, turn the crumpets over, and cook for a further 3 minutes until golden. Serve warm with butter.

Scotch Pancakes

Makes about 16

These pancakes – also known as drop scones – make a delicious tea-time treat when buttered and served with home-made jam. Alternatively, you can serve them as a pudding, topped with fruit and cream.

2 medium eggs
300 ml/½ pint milk
225 g/8 oz self-raising flour
a pinch of salt
55 g/2 oz caster sugar

1. Whisk together the eggs and milk in a large bowl, then beat in the flour, salt and sugar until you have a smooth batter. Alternatively, measure all the ingredients into a processor fitted with the metal blade and blend together.

2. To cook the drop scones, take about a tablespoon or less of the batter at a time, and let it drop from the spoon on to a gently heated non-stick surface, such as a large frying pan or a griddle. Spread the mixture out a little with the spoon to make a circle 5–7.5 cm/2–3 in across.

3. Cook the scones for about 30 seconds on the first side, a little less on the second. It is time to turn them when bubbles begin to form round the edges. If you can flip them over at this stage, you should get a second rise and a nice spongy result. Allow to cool on a wire rack.

Lancashire Potato Cakes

Makes about 13 – a baker's dozen!

I can remember my mother making these when we came in cold and wet from sledging. They cost very little, particularly if you have some leftover mashed potato. Eat them hot, as we did, almost straight from the pan, with a bit of melted butter on top.

225 g/8 oz cold mashed potato
55 g/2 oz butter or margarine, softened
175 g/6 oz self-raising flour
½ teaspoon salt
1 tablespoon full cream milk

1. Place all the ingredients except for the milk in a large bowl and mix together with a fork until you have an even, crumbly mixture.

2. Add the milk to bring it together into a dough.

3. Roll out on to a floured surface to a thickness of no more than 1 cm/½ in, then cut out rounds with an 8 cm/3 in fluted cutter. You will initially get about nine rounds, so push together the leftovers and re-roll to get the last three or so.

4. Place a griddle or a flat-based, non-stick pan over a low heat and, when it is hot, toast the potato cakes in batches, cooking them for 1 minute or so on each side until they are a mottled, golden brown. I find it easiest to flip them over with a fish slice. They will rise slightly during the cooking process.

Singin' Hinnies

Makes 12

The name of these Geordie scones comes, I am told, from the cook saying you could hear them 'singing, honey', as they were cooking on the griddle.

350 g/12 oz self-raising flour
1 teaspoon salt
55 g/2 oz ground rice
55 g/2 oz granulated sugar
25 g/1 oz margarine
85 g/3 oz currants
300 ml/½ pint milk

1. Measure the flour, salt, ground rice and sugar into a bowl, then rub in the margarine with your fingertips until the mixture resembles fine breadcrumbs.

2. Mix in the currants, then add most of the milk – but not all at once, as sometimes, depending on the flour, you don't need as much as I have given. You require just enough to bring the mixture together into a soft dough that is not too sticky.

3. Roll out the dough on a floured surface to a thickness of about 1 cm/½ in. Cut into squares and then triangles, and prick all over with a fork.

4. Place a griddle or a flat-based, non-stick pan over a gentle heat. Using a spatula or fish slice to lift the triangles on to the heated griddle, cook for about 3 minutes on each side until golden brown. Serve immediately, with honey if you wish.

Waffles

Makes about 10

You may have an electric machine that can be adapted to make waffles, or just an old-fashioned waffle iron that you heat on the stove top. Whichever, follow the manufacturer's instructions before you pour in the batter.

450 ml/16 fl oz skimmed milk
75 ml/2½ fl oz vegetable oil
2 large eggs
225 g/8 oz self-raising flour
½ teaspoon salt
1 tablespoon caster sugar

1. You can make this batter in a processor fitted with the metal blade by first mixing the milk, oil and eggs together, then pouring the dry ingredients down the funnel as the machine is running. Alternatively, whisk together the eggs, oil and milk in a bowl and then, in a separate and larger bowl, mix together the flour, salt and sugar. Make a well in the centre and pour in the egg mixture, then beat together until you have a smooth batter.

2. Heat your waffle iron or machine and grease it if it is non-stick. Then pour in enough batter to cover one surface well, allowing a little room for expansion. Close and cook for 3–4 minutes on one side, then turn over the waffle iron and cook for the same length of time on the other side. Best served warm, with butter and maple syrup.

CHOCOLATE HEAVEN

The downfall of many a diet, chocolate must be the world's most popular sweet flavouring, and not surprisingly, since it actually contains a substance which helps to raise the spirits. And if the way to a man's heart is through his stomach, then I think a good chocolate cake is one of the quickest ways of getting there. It's certainly as seductive as a candle-lit dinner.

It's important when buying bars of chocolate for cooking to check the percentage of cocoa solids they contain. Some very popular brands have only 35 per cent, and although this will give a reasonable result, the slightly more expensive chocolate that contains around 70 per cent cocoa solids will give a much richer, more chocolatey taste.

The most usual cause of problems when cooking with chocolate is over-heating. If you melt it in a heatproof bowl set over a pan of hot water, don't let the water come into contact with the bowl, and keep it to barely simmering. You don't need boiling heat. Lots of people melt it in the microwave, which is fine so long as yours doesn't have any obvious hot spots. Again, take it gently, using short bursts of a lower power.

I make no apology for including the recipe for chocolate courgette cake here, though many *This Morning* viewers will already have it. It remains the most popular one we ever did, and I still sometimes get letters from people saying they have lost their original copy or lent it and not got it back, and can I please send another – ten years later!

Chocolate Courgette Cake

Makes 1 x 20 cm/8 in cake

This makes a lovely moist cake, and is a particularly useful way of using up a glut of courgettes. It tastes even better the next day, but I can't tell you how long it lasts because it's so popular, it all gets eaten up very quickly!

175 g/6 oz plain chocolate
2 large eggs
175 ml/6 fl oz vegetable oil
200 g/7 oz self-raising flour
½ teaspoon salt
115 g/4 oz caster sugar
225 g/8 oz peeled weight courgettes, grated
55 g/2 oz walnuts, chopped

1. Preheat the oven to 180°C/350°F/Gas 4. Grease and flour a 20 cm/8 in round cake tin.

2. Melt the chocolate in a bowl set over a pan of barely simmering water or in a microwave (see page 81), and set aside.

3. In a large bowl, whisk together the eggs and oil.

4. Measure the flour, salt and sugar into another bowl, and mix together. Gradually add this mixture to the whisked egg and oil, and beat well together.

5. Stir in the melted chocolate, then the grated courgettes and nuts. Mix well and pour into the prepared cake tin. Bake for 1 hour or until the cake is well risen, and is firm and springy to the touch in the centre. Allow to cool in the tin for 10 minutes before turning out on to a wire rack.

NOTE *If desired, the cake can be sandwiched or covered with butter icing flavoured with cocoa, see page 126.*

Sachertorte –
The Ultimate Chocolate Cake

Makes 1 x 20cm/8 in round cake

This classic chocolate cake, which comes from Austria, is rich but light.

100 g/3½ oz dark chocolate, broken
into pieces
115 g/4 oz slightly salted butter
115 g/4 oz caster sugar
6 medium eggs, separated
115 g/4 oz plain flour, sifted
3–4 tablespoons apricot jam

For the icing
200 g/7 oz dark chocolate, broken into
pieces
150 ml/¼ pint double cream
115 g/4 oz icing sugar, sifted

1. Preheat the oven to 180°C/350°F/Gas 4 and grease and base-line a 20 cm/8 in round cake tin.

2. Melt the chocolate for the cake in a bowl set over a pan of barely simmering water, then allow to cool a little. Alternatively, use a microwave (see page 81).

3. Cream the butter with 75 g/3 oz of the sugar in a bowl by beating it until light and fluffy. Beat in the egg yolks and cooled, melted chocolate. Fold in the flour.

4. In a separate bowl, whisk the egg whites until they form stiff peaks. Then gradually whisk in the remaining sugar until stiff and glossy.

5. Stir a spoonful of egg white into the chocolate mixture, then fold in the rest with a metal spoon.

6. Spoon into the prepared cake tin, and bake for 1–1¼ hours until springy to a touch in the centre, or a skewer inserted in the middle comes out clean. Leave to cool in the tin for a few minutes before turning out on to a wire rack.

7. When cooled, cut the cake through the centre and sandwich together with the apricot jam.

8. Make the icing by melting the chocolate as before. Allow to cool, then fold in the cream, followed by the icing sugar. The mixture will thicken as it cools, and, when it is thick enough to coat the back of a wooden spoon, pour it over the cake. Smooth over the top and sides with a palette knife or spatula.

NOTE *This cake is often served with whipped cream.*

Swedish Easter Cake

Makes 1 x 20 cm/8 in cake

This chocolate, orange and marzipan treat is a great favourite when served as a pudding. Decorate each slice with a few strawberries or raspberries and serve with a coulis (a sweetened fruit purée). It is easier to grate both the marzipan and the chocolate if they have first been chilled in the fridge.

400 g/14 oz marzipan
4 large eggs, beaten
a scant 50 ml/2 fl oz orange juice
115 g/4 oz dark chocolate

1. Preheat the oven to 200°C/400°F/Gas 6. Grease, flour, and base line an 20 cm/8 in solid cake tin or flan dish – don't use a loose-bottomed one, or the runny mixture will seep out.

2. Grate the marzipan into a bowl, and blend it with the eggs and orange juice until it is smooth and fluffy. Alternatively, blend in a processor.

3. Pour the mixture into the prepared tin. Bake for 30 minutes, or until set and golden.

4. Allow the cake to cool in the tin, for a couple of minutes only, while you grate the chocolate. Loosen round the edges with a knife, then turn out on to a serving plate and peel away the paper from the base. Spread the grated chocolate over the cake while it is still warm, so that some of it melts into the cake. When cool, serve in slices either as it is, or with summer fruits as suggested above.

Chocolate Suicide

Makes 16 triangles

100 g/3½ oz plain chocolate, broken into pieces
150 g/5 oz butter
1 teaspoon orange oil (or grated zest of an orange)
200 g/7 oz caster sugar
100 g/3½ oz plain flour
25 g/1 oz cocoa powder
3 large eggs
175 g/6 oz crème fraîche

For the icing
100 g/3½ oz white chocolate, broken into pieces
2 tablespoons crème fraîche

1. Preheat the oven to 180°C/350°F/Gas 4, and line a 30 x 20 cm/12 x 8 in Swiss roll tin with baking parchment.

2. Melt the chocolate together with the butter in a heat proof bowl placed over a pan of barely simmering water or in a microwave.

3. When melted, spoon into the bowl of a processor fitted with the metal blade. Add all the other ingredients and process for 10 seconds.

4. Pour into the lined Swiss roll tin, and bake for 30 minutes or until a skewer inserted in the centre comes out clean.

5. Allow the cake to cool in the tin, then peel away the baking parchment. Cut into largeish squares, and then halve these across into triangles.

6. To ice, melt the white chocolate in a bowl set over a pan of barely simmering water or in a microwave. Combine with the crème fraîche and spread or drizzle over the top of each triangle.

Florentines

Makes 30–40

115 g/4 oz butter
85 g/3 oz caster sugar
1 tablespoon double cream
115 g/4 oz flaked almonds
55 g/2 oz chopped candied peel or raisins
55 g/2 oz glacé cherries, quartered
175 g/6 oz plain or white chocolate

1. Preheat the oven to 180°C/350°F/Gas 4.

2. Melt the butter in a pan over a gentle heat, then add the sugar. Continue to heat gently, stirring until the sugar dissolves. Add the cream, bring the mixture up to the boil, and bubble gently for 1 minute, stirring all the time.

3. Add the nuts, peel or raisins and the cherries to the mixture, and mix together well. Using two teaspoons, put small amounts on to baking trays lined with baking parchment. Leave plenty of room for them to spread.

4. Bake for 5–8 minutes until just golden. Remove from the oven and, using a spatula, push the florentines into neat little rounds. Allow to cool on the trays.

5. Meanwhile, melt the chocolate in a bowl set over a pan of barely simmering water, or in a microwave (see page 81). When the florentines are cool, coat the bottom of each one with the melted chocolate. Leave to set on non-stick baking parchment.

Chocolate Orange Truffle Torte

Makes 1 x 22 cm/9 in torte

Use good quality chocolate which has a high percentage of cocoa solids (ideally 70 per cent) – it's more expensive, but definitely worth it. If you can't get orange oil, you could use a few drops of orange essence flavouring instead.

2 chocolate flakes
450 g/1 lb dark chocolate, broken into pieces
4 tablespoons orange liqueur (e.g. Cointreau, Curaçao)
2 tablespoons orange oil
4 tablespoons golden syrup
600 ml/1 pint double cream

1. Line a 22 cm/9 in round cake tin with cling film – this enables you to turn out the torte when it is set. Crumble the chocolate flakes into small pieces with your fingers, and scatter over the lined base.

2. Melt the chocolate, liqueur, orange oil and golden syrup in a heatproof bowl set over a pan of barely simmering water. When the chocolate has melted, and the sauce is smooth, remove from the heat. Pour into another bowl and leave to cool for a few minutes.

3. Meanwhile, in another bowl, whisk the cream until thick and just holding its shape. Fold the cream into the slightly cooled chocolate mixture, then pour into the cake tin over the crumbed base. Place in the fridge to set for several hours, or overnight.

4. When ready to serve, turn out the torte on to a serving plate, and carefully peel away the film. Smooth the sides with a knife or spatula to finish neatly.

NOTE *The cake keeps for several days in the fridge, so is a useful recipe to prepare in advance for a party. I serve it in slices with a little crème fraîche.*

Baked White Chocolate Cheesecake

Makes 2 x 20 cm/8 in round cheesecakes
or 1 x 25 x 20 cm/10 x 8 in rectangular cake

I usually make two round cakes rather than one large rectangular one, and freeze one for an emergency!
You can always finish one with crumbled white chocolate flake, instead of making the curls.

For the base	For the filling	For the topping
85 g/3 oz butter	280 g/10 oz white chocolate,	175 g/6 oz white chocolate,
280 g/10 oz chocolate-coated	broken into pieces	broken into pieces
wholemeal biscuits	55 g/2 oz butter, softened	450 ml/16 fl oz double
	450 g/1 lb cream cheese	cream, whipped
	55 g/2 oz caster sugar	a little cocoa powder,
	2 large eggs, beaten	for dusting

1. Preheat the oven to 160°C/325°F/Gas 3 and lightly grease the tin or tins.

2. To make the base, melt the butter in a pan, and finely crumb the biscuits (this is most easily done in a processor). Mix the melted butter and crumbs together and press into the base of the tin or tins, smoothing with a spatula. Chill in the fridge while making the filling.

3. Melt the white chocolate for the filling in a bowl set over a pan of barely simmering water (see page 81). In a processor fitted with the metal blade, or in a warmed bowl, cream together the softened butter, cream cheese and sugar. Add the melted white chocolate and the beaten eggs. When well mixed, pour over the chilled base or bases.

4. Bake for 45 minutes or until the filling is golden brown and just set. Leave to cool in the tin. The cheesecake will rise as it cooks, but fall in the centre as it cools. If you are planning to freeze the cake, do so now, before adding the topping.

5. To make the topping, melt the white chocolate. Stir until smooth, then spread in a thin layer over a marble slab or metal baking tray, and leave to cool. Using a palette knife, press down at an acute angle on the chocolate and draw the blade across to form curls.

6. When you are ready to serve the cheesecake, transfer it from the tin (or tins) to a serving dish or plate. Spread the whipped cream over the top, and then scatter over the white chocolate curls. Finally, lightly dust with a little sieved cocoa powder.

10 COOKING WITH KIDS

It's going to be messy, but it's also going to be a lot of fun for all concerned. Resign yourself to hosing down the kitchen floor, as well as the kids, when you've finished, and get stuck in and enjoy it.

We had a great day cooking with Sophie and Duncan for the *This Morning* film, and they were able to go home with a box of goodies for mum or dad to try, even though they were only aged five. If you tailor your recipe ideas to the age of the children concerned, giving them something simple to start with, such as the chocolate crispies, they will be encouraged by early success and they can then try the more advanced stuff.

Do please take care when planning a session with children; the kitchen can be a dangerous place. Never leave children in the kitchen alone. Always be there to supervise. Keep very young children away from hot pans and ovens, and make sure they don't use sharp knives or equipment that could hurt them. It is a question really of suiting the recipe to the ability of the child, and you should find something in this chapter to suit a range of ages and abilities.

It would be a pity if the cooking and baking skills that my generation learnt at 'our mother's knee' were to disappear. We live in an age where there are more working mums, and many more ready-made and takeaway meals. There are fewer cookery lessons in school than there used to be, too, which makes it all the more important to set to and have a session with the kids. It will almost certainly be cheaper than a day out at an amusement park, and will provide happy memories and a sense of achievement for all of you.

Lamingtons

Makes 12

You can use any plain sponge cake for this, bought or home-made. A large rectangular sponge of about 28 x 20 cm/11 x 8 in is ideal. You may have to buy two smaller ones.

Plain sponge, cut into small rectangles or squares

For the chocolate icing
55 g/2 oz butter
55 g/2 oz cocoa powder
6 tablespoons just boiled water
a few drops of vanilla extract
375 g/13 oz icing sugar, sifted
225 g/8 oz desiccated coconut

1. Gently heat the butter in a small pan until just melted or use a microwave.

2. Dissolve the cocoa in the just boiled water, and mix with the butter. Mix in the vanilla, then gradually stir in the icing sugar, and beat well – the consistency should be fairly runny.

3. Coat the rectangles or squares of sponge with the icing either by placing the pieces of cake on a wire rack with something underneath to catch the drips, and then pouring over the icing, or by holding each piece on a fork and dipping it into the icing bowl. When the icing has soaked into the cake, roll each piece in coconut to coat. Leave to dry on a wire rack.

Chocolate Tiles

Makes 12

For the base
200 g/7 oz plain chocolate, broken into pieces
175 g/6 oz butter
200 g/7 oz broken biscuits
115 g/4 oz chopped mixed nuts
115 g/4 oz raisins

For the topping
115 g/4 oz plain chocolate
115 g/4 oz milk chocolate

1. Melt the chocolate and butter together, either in a bowl set over a pan of barely simmering water or in a microwave (see page 81).

2. Crumb the biscuits, either in a processor or by placing them in a plastic bag and crushing with a rolling pin. Add to the melted chocolate and mix well. Add the nuts and raisins and mix well.

3. Press the base mixture into an 28 x 20 cm/11 x 8 in baking tin lined with foil and smooth the top. Chill in the fridge until firm.

4. Separately melt the two chocolates for the topping, either in bowls set over barely simmering water or in a microwave. Pour over the base so that they produce a marbled effect. Chill in the fridge until the chocolate is set, then cut into squares.

*Lamingtons (p93), butterfly
buns (p97) and chocolate tiles*

Chocolate Crispies

Makes 8–10

These can be made with any suitable cereal. Many people like to use cornflakes, but I think rice crispies are nicer.

115 g/4 oz milk chocolate
3 mugs rice crispies or cornflakes

1. Melt the milk chocolate, either in a bowl set over a pan of barely simmering water or in a microwave (see page 81).

2. Pour in two mugs of rice crispies, and stir to coat. Add another mug of rice crispies and mix well, though avoid crushing the cereal. All the cereal should be covered in chocolate – add more if you think the chocolate can take it.

3. Have ready a bun tray filled with paper cases and use two spoons to transfer the chocolate-coated crispies to the cases. Remember that so long as chocolate touches chocolate, it will stick together as it cools. Leave to cool. Enjoy.

Quick Chocolate Truffles

Makes about 24

The cake can either be bought, or you can use home-made cake which has gone stale. Truffles look particularly nice in shiny, rather than paper, petits fours cases.

1 x 16 cm/6¼ in round chocolate cake
1 heaped tablespoon ground almonds
1 heaped tablespoon icing sugar
1 tablespoon orange juice
cocoa powder and chocolate vermicelli
for decorating
small petits fours cases for serving

1. Crumb the cake into a large bowl. Add the ground almonds, icing sugar and orange juice. Mix well and form into small balls.

2. Roll each ball in the cocoa and vermicelli to decorate. Place in the petits fours cases and refrigerate until ready to eat. They should keep for a week or more.

Butterfly Buns

Makes 12

115 g/4 oz soft margarine
115 g/4 oz caster sugar
115 g/4 oz white self-raising flour
2 medium eggs

For the icing
55 g/2 oz soft margarine or softened butter
1 teaspoon vanilla extract
3 heaped tablespoons icing sugar

1. Preheat the oven to 190°C/375°F/Gas 5.

2. Measure all the bun ingredients into a large bowl. Mix with a wooden spoon until you have a smooth batter that just drops off the spoon when you hold it up.

3. Line a bun tray with paper cases and divide the mixture between them – I find this easiest to do using two teaspoons.

4. Bake for about 15 minutes, or until the buns are golden brown and springy to the touch. Turn out and cool on a wire rack.

5. Meanwhile, make the icing by creaming together the margarine or butter, the vanilla extract and icing sugar in a bowl. When the buns are cool, make the 'butterflies' by cutting a round or 'lid' in the top of each bun with a sloping knife. Fill the holes with the icing and cut the lids you removed in half. Stand them on top of the icing in each hole to make the shape of a butterfly's wings.

NOTE *Without the wings these are fairy cakes. Once they are cool you can cover the top with a simple icing (recipe on page 126).*

Gingerbread Biscuits

Makes 20–30 shapes

Older children can make the dough with supervision and younger ones will enjoy cutting out the gingerbread shapes. These biscuits are called lebkuchen *in Austria, from where I got the recipe, and there they make them into decorated shapes to hang on the Christmas tree. They will last for more than a year if you increase the amount of flour in the recipe by 85–115 g/3–4 oz (although this makes them harder to roll out) and keep them in a dry place.*

175 g/6 oz soft brown sugar
2 tablespoons water
2 tablespoons orange juice
4 tablespoons golden syrup
2 tablespoons black treacle
200 g/7 oz butter, cut into pieces
675 g/1½ lb plain white flour
1 level teaspoon bicarbonate of soda

2 level teaspoons ground ginger
2 level teaspoons ground cinnamon

To finish
a little beaten egg
apricot jam and glacé fruit and
almonds to decorate, optional
white icing and silver balls, optional

1. Measure the sugar, water, orange juice, golden syrup and treacle into a large pan. Heat gently until the sugar has melted, then bring just up to a boil. Take off the heat, add the butter, and stir until the butter has melted.

2. In a separate bowl, mix together the flour, bicarbonate of soda, ground ginger and cinnamon. Beat into the butter and sugar mixture until you have a smooth, slightly runny dough. Chill in the fridge for at least 30 minutes.

3. When firm, roll out the dough on to a well floured surface to a thickness of about 5 mm/¼ inch. If the dough is too sticky to roll out, add a little more flour and knead it in until you get a consistency that you can roll.

4. Use biscuit cutters of whatever shape you fancy to cut out shapes, and transfer them to baking trays lined with baking parchment. You can gather up the leftovers and re-roll to make more. Brush with a little beaten egg for a shiny finish and bake for 15 minutes in an oven preheated to 180°C/350°F/Gas 4. Allow to cool a little on the trays before lifting off on to a wire rack.

5. Traditionally, these biscuits are glazed with warm, sieved apricot jam, which also acts as a sort of edible glue to fix on pieces of glacé fruit or almonds. You could pipe white icing round the edges and, if you have made stars or Christmas trees, you could add silver balls.

11 | WARM TEA-TIME TREATS

All the pleasures of afternoon tea – coming home on a cold day to a cup of tea by the fire and something warm, tasty and comforting to go with it – is the feel of this chapter. It is a meal that has almost gone out of fashion, and yet if you are eating late for some reason, it is such a good bridge between lunch and supper, in fact almost essential if stomach rumblings are not to spoil your enjoyment of an evening out!

Nearly all the recipes here are ones that are best served fresh, warm from the oven. If you have to save things until the next day, some can be revived by warming them through in a low oven again.

If your scones are more like rock cakes, it may be that you are making the mixture too dry, or rolling it out too thin. It takes time and a bit of practice to get them just how they should be, so persevere – remember that you have to learn any skill, and will improve as you go on.

Pineapple Upside-down Triangles

Makes 8

25 g/1 oz butter
25 g/1 oz soft brown sugar
2 tablespoons juice from the can of pineapple
4 canned pineapple rings
4 glacé cherries

For the cakey pastry
85 g/3 oz white self-raising flour
85 g/3 oz wholemeal self-raising flour
85 g/3 oz butter, cold from the fridge
1 level dessertspoon caster sugar
a pinch of salt
1 large egg

1. Preheat the oven to 200°C/400°F/Gas 6.

2. In a small pan, melt the butter and sugar together with the pineapple juice. Pour into a 23 cm/9 in square cake tin with a solid base – if you use a loose-bottomed one, the mixture will leak out. Arrange the four rings of pineapple on top, and place a glacé cherry in the centre of each ring.

3. Make the cakey pastry by placing all the ingredients, except the egg, in a processor fitted with the metal blade and then, with the motor still running, drop in the egg. It will quickly come together into a ball.

4. Press out the dough with your hands on a floured surface to make a square shape the size of the tin you have used. Lift it over the fruit base and press down to cover – any spare bits can be tucked in.

5. Bake for 30 minutes or until the pastry is crisp and golden.

6. Allow to cool in the tin for 5 minutes, then loosen around the edges with a knife, and turn out upside down on to a serving plate. Cut into quarters, then cut each of these diagonally into a triangle. Serve warm, with or without thick cream.

Spiced Barm Brack

Makes 1 x 18 cm/7 in round loaf

Barm is the froth that collects on fermenting malt liquor, which in the past was used instead of yeast to raise dough. The Celtic word 'brack' means speckled, which this is, with fruits and spices. You can eat it freshly sliced, with butter warmly melting on top, or toast it the next day.

450 g/1 lb strong white flour
15 g/½ oz fresh yeast plus
½ teaspoon sugar,
or 1 x 6 g sachet easy blend yeast
275 ml/9½ fl oz warm milk and water
(half and half)
25 g/1 oz butter, cut into pieces
1 teaspoon mixed spice

1 teaspoon ground nutmeg
55 g/2 oz soft brown sugar
225 g/8 oz sultanas
55 g/2 oz mixed candied peel

To glaze
1 tablespoon caster sugar
1 tablespoon water

1. Measure the flour into a large bowl. If using fresh yeast, combine it with the sugar and the warm water and milk in a bowl or jug. Leave to stand for 10 minutes until it becomes frothy. If using dried easy blend yeast, mix it in with the flour.

2. Rub the butter into the flour with your fingertips, as in pastry making. Stir in the mixed spice, nutmeg, brown sugar, sultanas and candied peel, and make a well in the centre. Pour in the warm milk and water (or the fresh yeast mixture) and mix with a wooden spoon or your hand to make a firm dough. As different flours absorb different amounts of water, you may need to add a little more warm water.

3. Turn out on to a floured surface and knead for about 10 minutes until the dough is smooth and elastic. Put into a lightly greased large bowl, cover with either a damp tea towel or cling film, and leave to rise in a warm place for at least 1 hour until doubled in size. 'Knock back' the dough by punching it to redistribute the air, then shape it into a greased 18 cm/7 inch cake tin. Cover again and leave in a warm place to rise for a further hour or so. Preheat the oven to 200°C/400°F/Gas 6. Bake for 35 minutes.

4. Meanwhile, make the glaze by dissolving the sugar and water in a small pan over a low heat. Bring up to the boil, and boil for a minute or so, then brush over the top of the loaf. Return it to the oven for a further 5 minutes. Then take the loaf out and let it stand in the tin for just a minute or two before turning it out on to a wire rack to cool.

*Scones (p108) and
spiced barm brack*

Wholemeal Apple and Yoghurt Farls

Makes 8

225g/8 oz wholemeal self-raising flour
1 teaspoon baking powder
1 tablespoon caster sugar
55g/2 oz butter or margarine, cut into pieces
55g/2 oz chopped walnuts
1 medium dessert apple
150 ml/5 fl oz carton natural yoghurt

1. Preheat the oven to 220°C/425°F/Gas 7.

2. Measure the flour, baking powder and caster sugar into a large bowl. Rub in the butter or margarine with your fingertips until the mixture resembles fine breadcrumbs.

3. Add the chopped nuts, then peel the apple. Grate it into the bowl, turning it as you grate so as to waste as little as possible, and mix in with a fork.

4. Mix in the yoghurt with the fork, adding a little water, if necessary, to get a soft but not sticky dough.

5. Turn out the dough on to a floured surface and knead into a neat round. Roll out with a floured rolling pin into a circle with a thickness of 2 cm/¾ in. Transfer this to a greased baking tray and, with the back of a knife, mark into eight 'farls' – as if you were marking the slices of a cake – by almost, but not quite, cutting through the dough.

6. Bake for about 15 minutes. It is done if it sounds hollow when you tap it on the base. Cool on a rack and break into the slices or 'farls' before eating as it is, or buttered and spread with honey.

Pine Nut and Cream Cheesecakes

Makes 2 x 20 cm/8 in cakes

As this recipe makes two cakes, it's one I often use when I need to give a cake to a friend, or if someone has asked me to bake for a cake stall. I don't find giving one away a problem, it's the complaints I get from the family about the house smelling of baking and them not being able to eat anything – safer to make two! It's also a good cake for those who don't have a very sweet tooth, since it has an almost savoury taste.

55 g/2 oz butter, softened
175 g/6 oz caster sugar
200 g/7 oz self-raising flour
1 tablespoon clear honey
grated zest of an orange or a lemon
450 g/1 lb cream cheese
5 medium eggs, separated
115 g/4 oz pine nuts, lightly toasted

1. Preheat the oven to 160°C/325°F/Gas 3, and grease and flour two 20 cm/8 inch round cake tins.

2. Cream the butter and sugar together in a large bowl. Add a spoonful of flour to stop the mixture curdling, then beat in the honey, orange or lemon zest and the cream cheese, a quarter at a time. Add the egg yolks one by one, beating well, then gently mix in the remaining flour and the pine nuts.

3. In another large bowl, whisk the egg whites until they make stiff peaks. Fold in the cream cheese mixture. Divide this mixture between the two tins and smooth over the tops.

4. Bake for 1½ hours until well risen and golden brown on top. Rather than take the cakes out, however, it is best to leave them to cool in the turned-off oven – they will sink a bit in the middle, but less than if taken out to cool.

NOTE *These cakes freeze well, wrapped in cling film, and, when de-frosted, are delicious if warmed a little before being served in slices, with a little icing sugar sifted over, or decorated with strips of orange or lemon peel. Use a zester to remove thin strips of orange or lemon peel without the pith and put in a pan with a little water and sugar. Bring up to the boil and simmer together for 10 minutes. Lift out, drain, and use when dry as a decoration.*

Love Cake

Serves 2 hearty appetites (4 if you choose to share)

Love cake is made with simple ingredients, and is something that, in the past, a girl might have made to take along if she were walking out with a man – just so he would know that he would get fed all right if they were to wed.

200 g/7 oz self-raising flour
25 g/1 oz cornflour
a good pinch of salt
25 g/1 oz caster sugar
25 g/1 oz butter, cut into pieces
150 ml/¼ pint milk
2 tablespoons strawberry jam

1. Preheat the oven to 220°C/425°F/Gas 7.

2. Measure the flour, cornflour, salt and sugar into a large bowl, and rub in the butter, as in making pastry.

3. Gradually add the milk to give you a soft dough – it should not need all of it. Keep a little for brushing over later. Turn out on to a floured surface, knead lightly, and roll out to a rectangle of about 50 x 20 cm/20 x 8 in.

4. Spread the dough with the jam, roll up along the longest side, as for a Swiss roll, and place on a greased baking tray. Form the roll into a rough heart shape by bringing the ends together to make a point at the bottom – join them with a little of the milk to make them stick – and curve inwards at the top. With a pair of scissors, make a pattern of small V-shaped cuts around the top, then brush the top with the rest of the milk.

5. Bake for 15 minutes, or until the cake is golden brown and sounds hollow when tapped on the bottom.

Scones

Makes about 8

225 g/8 oz self-raising flour
1 teaspoon baking powder
55 g/2 oz caster sugar
55 g/2 oz butter or margarine, cut into pieces
1 medium egg
a little milk

1. Preheat the oven to 220°C/425°F/Gas 7.

2. Sift the flour and baking powder into a bowl. Add the sugar and butter or margarine, and rub in with your fingertips until the mixture resembles fine breadcrumbs.

3. Whisk the egg lightly with a fork in a small bowl, and add to the mixture with just enough milk to form a soft dough.

4. Roll out on a floured board to a thickness of about 4 cm/1½ in. Cut out rounds with a small cutter, taking care not to twist the cutter as this can lead to uneven shapes when baked.

5. Place the rounds on a lightly greased baking tray, and bake for 10–15 minutes, until risen and golden brown.

6. Leave the scones to cool on a rack, then split horizontally and serve with strawberry jam and thick cream.

VARIATIONS *Add 55 g/2 oz chopped glacé cherries, or currants, or chopped nuts.*

Hot Cross Buns

Makes 12

We think of hot cross buns at Easter time as having the Christian symbol of the cross on them, but it seems to be an adaptation of an older pagan symbol – the circle of the sun cut by a cross into the four seasons. The golden colour of the baked dough is important too, symbolizing the yellow colours of the new life bursting forth in spring – daffodils and primroses, as well as yellow egg yolks, eggs being another potent Easter tradition.

450 g/1 lb strong plain flour
85 g/3 oz butter, cut into pieces
1 sachet (6 g) easy blend dried yeast
1 teaspoon salt
1 teaspoon ground cinnamon
1 teaspoon mixed spice
1 teaspoon grated nutmeg
55 g/2 oz caster sugar
85 g/3 oz currants
25 g/1 oz mixed candied peel

1 large egg, beaten
300 ml/½ pint warm milk
55 g/2 oz plain flour
a little cold water

For the glaze
3 tablespoons caster sugar
2 tablespoons milk
2 tablespoons water

1. Sift the strong plain flour into a warm mixing bowl, and rub in the butter, as in pastry making. Stir in the yeast, salt, spices, sugar, currants and candied peel, mixing well. Stir in the egg, and then gradually add the warm milk to make a smooth dough – as different flours absorb different amounts of liquid, you may or may not need all of the milk.

2. Turn out the dough on to a floured surface and knead for 5 minutes until it is smooth and elastic. If it becomes a bit sticky, add more flour. Divide the dough into twelve, smooth into rounds and place on a lightly oiled baking tray. Cover with a clean tea towel and leave to rise in a warm place for about 1 hour until doubled in size.

3. Make a stiff dough with 55 g/2 oz plain flour and a little cold water. Roll out thinly on a floured surface and cut into strips to make crosses. Fix the crosses to the risen buns with a little water.

4. Preheat the oven to 200°C/400°F/Gas 6. Bake for 15–20 minutes until the buns are golden brown and sound hollow when tapped on the bottom. Cool on a wire rack.

5. To make the glaze, gently heat the sugar, milk and water in a small pan until the sugar is dissolved. Bring to the boil and boil for a couple of minutes. Brush this warm glaze over each bun twice. Serve warm, or split and toasted then spread with butter and honey.

12 | ROLL 'EM UP

If you are wondering whether a roulade is just a posh name for a Swiss roll, the difference, as far as I am concerned, is that roulade mixtures don't contain any flour. As a result, they are very useful if you know someone who is on a gluten-, or wheat-free diet, just so long, of course, as there is no wheat in the filling either. I have also found that a roulade can be a nice vegetarian option.

They can be served either hot or cold, and you will find here both sweet and savoury ideas. The tricky bit is the rolling up. Do invest in some baking parchment, which is non-stick, and strong enough to hold everything firmly and act as a guide when you are rolling. Try always to end up with the join underneath; it will not only look neater, but will hold together better. And if your roulade cracks a bit when you're rolling out, well, that just adds to the home-made appeal, doesn't it?

Black Forest Roulade (p117)

Luscious Lemon Roll

Serves 6–8

This fatless sponge doesn't keep well, so it is best to eat it the same day, or the next. If you want it to keep for a few days, add 25 g/1 oz melted butter at the same stage as the flour, although be aware that this will make it a little less light.

3 large eggs
115 g/4 oz caster sugar
1 tablespoon lemon juice
finely grated zest of a lemon
85 g/3 oz self-raising flour
a little extra caster sugar for sprinkling
a small jar (320 g/11½ oz) lemon curd

1. Preheat the oven to 200°C/400°F/Gas 6.

2. Whisk together the eggs and caster sugar in a large bowl until thick enough to leave a ribbon-like trail on the surface for a second or two when you lift the whisk.

3. Add the lemon juice and zest, sift in the flour, and fold together with a metal spoon. Pour into a 33 x 23 cm/13 x 9 in Swiss roll tin lined with baking parchment. Bake for 10 minutes until golden brown and springy to the touch.

4. Allow the cake to cool in the tin for no more than a couple of minutes (you won't be able to roll it up unless it is still warm), then loosen the paper round the edges and tip out on to a sheet of greaseproof paper that has been dredged with caster sugar. Carefully peel away the baking parchment from the bottom of the cake, and daub with blobs of lemon curd, spreading them evenly together to cover. Using the greaseproof paper as a guide, roll up the cake from the narrow end, leaving the join on the underside.

Orange and Pistachio Swiss Roll

Serves 6–8

4 large eggs, separated
115 g/4 oz caster sugar
115 g/4 oz pistachio nuts, finely chopped
⅛ teaspoon cream of tartar
⅛ teaspoon salt
icing sugar for dusting

For the filling
300 ml/½ pint whipping cream
1 tablespoon caster sugar
grated zest of 1 orange
2–3 drops orange oil
1 tablespoon orange liqueur

1. Preheat the oven to 180°C/350°F/Gas 4.

2. Beat together the egg yolks and sugar in a bowl until thick, then stir in the pistachios. In a separate bowl, beat the egg whites with the cream of tartar and salt until they hold their peaks, then fold gently into the pistachio mixture.

3. Pour the mixture into a 30 x 24 cm/12 x 9½ in Swiss roll tin lined with baking parchment and bake for 15 minutes.

4. Turn the cake out on to a sheet of greaseproof paper dusted with icing sugar. Peel off the baking parchment and trim the edges until you have neat, straight sides. Roll up the cake, using the greaseproof paper to help you, while it is still warm. Leave to cool.

5. Whip the cream in a bowl until it holds soft peaks. Fold in the sugar and orange zest, then add the orange oil and orange liqueur. Gently unroll the cake, spread with the cream mixture, and re-roll on to a serving plate.

A Savoury Roulade for Christmas

Serves 4

For the herb crust	For the roulade	For the filling
40 g/1½ oz butter	275 ml/10 fl oz milk	285 g/10 oz parsnips, peeled
a bunch of spring onions,	25 g/1 oz plain flour	and cut into chunks
trimmed and chopped	40 g/1½ oz butter	25 g/1 oz butter
1 tablespoon chopped	3 large eggs, separated	2 tablespoons double cream
fresh parsley	115 g/4 oz Gouda cheese,	½ teaspoon grated nutmeg
2 teaspoons dried mixed herbs	grated	salt and pepper
85 g/3 oz brown		40 g/1½ oz freshly grated
breadcrumbs		Parmesan
salt and pepper		85 g/3 oz pine nuts, toasted

1. Preheat the oven to 200°C/400°F/Gas 6, and line a 32 x 23 cm/13 x 9 in Swiss roll tin with baking parchment.

2. To make the herb crust, melt the butter in a pan and gently fry the chopped spring onions for about 5 minutes. Add the parsley, mixed herbs and breadcrumbs, and combine to make a sort of loose stuffing mixture. Season to taste, and spread over the lining in the base of the tin.

3. To make the roulade, measure the milk and flour into a pan, and whisk together over a gentle heat until combined. Add the butter in two or three pieces and whisk until the sauce thickens. Cook gently for a couple of minutes, then remove from the heat and allow to cool slightly.

4. Beat the yolks into the slightly cooled sauce, mix in the grated cheese, and season to taste. In a clean bowl, whisk the egg whites until stiff. Mix a spoonful of egg white into the cheese sauce to loosen it, then carefully fold in the rest. Spread this evenly over the herb mixture in the tin, pushing it well into the corners. Bake for 25 minutes, or until it feels springy in the centre.

5. Meanwhile, make the filling by boiling the parsnips in salted water for about 15 minutes until done. Drain well. Add the butter, cream, grated nutmeg and seasoning, and mash or purée until smooth.

6. To assemble, lay a sheet of greaseproof paper, baking parchment or foil, slightly bigger than the tin, on your work surface and sprinkle with Parmesan. Turn the roulade out on to this, and remove the paper. Spread the parsnip mixture over the herb crust, which will now be on the top, and sprinkle over the pine nuts. Roll up along the longest edge and place on a serving dish with the join underneath.

NOTE *This is good served with a sauce made from 1 red onion and 115 g/4 oz cranberries – sauté sliced red onions in butter for 10 minutes until soft, add the cranberries, a glass of red wine, a spoonful of sugar and salt and pepper to taste. Simmer together until thickened.*

Rum Roll

Serves 6–8

This makes a more solid, crunchy roll than the usual lighter mixtures, and most people find it easier to make. For those who don't like the usual Christmas fruit cake, it can also be adapted into a chocolate log by covering it when filled and rolled with a double quantity of filling. Mark with a fork to look like rough bark, then melt 115 g/4 oz of chocolate and drizzle this over the top.

225 g/8 oz dark chocolate
25 g/1 oz butter
200 g/7 oz digestive biscuits, finely crumbed
85 g/3 oz plain cake crumbs
caster sugar for sprinkling

For the filling
55 g/2 oz butter
150 g/5 oz icing sugar
2 dessertspoons dark rum

1. Melt the chocolate and butter together in a heatproof bowl set over a pan of barely simmering water, and stir until smooth.

2. Stir in the biscuit and cake crumbs – I find it quickest and easiest to make these in a processor – and mix well to form a stiff ball of paste.

3. Sprinkle a 30 cm/12 in square of foil with the caster sugar. Roll out the ball of paste on this with a rolling pin to make a square a bit smaller all round than the foil.

4. Make the filling by softening the butter in a bowl and then beating in the other ingredients. Spread this over the square of paste. Use the foil to help you roll up the paste over the filling like a Swiss roll – the caster sugar should stop it sticking to the foil, as well as giving it a nice finish. Chill in the fridge until firm before serving sliced into circles.

Black Forest Roulade

Serves 6

The cherry pie filling can be bought ready-made from the supermarket.

175 g/6 oz plain chocolate, broken
into pieces
6 large eggs, separated
115 g/4 oz caster sugar, plus extra
for dusting
butter or sunflower oil for greasing

For the filling
115 g/4 oz Greek natural yoghurt
175g/6 oz cherry pie filling

2 tablespoons dessicated coconut
for decoration, optional

1. Preheat the oven to 180°C/350°F/Gas 4.

2. Melt the chocolate in a bowl set over a pan of barely simmering water (see page 81). When melted, stir gently until smooth, then remove from the heat.

3. Whisk the egg yolks, add the sugar, and continue whisking until pale and foamy. Stir in the melted chocolate and beat until smooth.

4. In a separate, clean bowl, and using a clean whisk, beat the whites until stiff – they won't stiffen sufficiently if there is even the tiniest bit of grease around. Fold the whites gently into the chocolate mixture.

5. Grease a 20 x 25 cm/8 x 10 in Swiss roll tin, and line with baking parchment. Pour in the roulade mixture and spread it evenly around the tin. Sprinkle the coconut over the surface, if using. Bake for 20 minutes. Remove the tin from the oven, cover with a damp tea towel and leave for 10 minutes.

6. Turn the sponge out on to a sheet of baking parchment that has been sprinkled with a little caster sugar, and carefully peel off the lining paper. Leave to cool slightly, then trim the cake so you have neat, straight edges. When almost cooled, spread the sponge with the yoghurt and then the cherry pie filling. Roll up, using the baking parchment to help you. Serve in slices.

Spinach Roulade

Makes 10 slices

15 g/½ oz butter, melted
450 g/1 lb frozen chopped spinach
(or see variations)
3 large eggs, separated

salt and pepper
freshy grated nutmeg
2 tablespoons freshly
grated Parmesan

1. Preheat the oven to 180°C/350°F/Gas 4. Line a 30 x 25 cm/12 x 10 in Swiss roll tin with baking parchment, and brush with a little of the melted butter.

2. Cook the spinach from frozen in a pan over gentle heat without a lid, to make sure it dries out as much as possible. When cooked, press through a sieve to extract any remaining water, and leave to cool in a bowl. Beat the egg yolks and the remaining melted butter into the spinach. Season generously with salt, pepper and grated nutmeg.

3. Whisk the egg whites until stiff. Stir a spoonful into the spinach mixture to slacken it, then fold in the rest of the egg whites. Spoon the mixture into the prepared tin. Spread it carefully into the corners and smooth the top. Bake for 15 minutes until just firm in the centre.

4. Meanwhile, spread another sheet of baking parchment, a little larger than the size of the tin, on a work surface, and scatter with Parmesan. When the roulade is cooked, loosen the edges with a knife and turn out on to the cheese-sprinkled paper. Carefully peel off the parchment.

5. If you are serving the roulade hot, cover it with your choice of filling and roll up while still warm. Use the paper on which you spread the cheese to help you, finishing with the join underneath. If you are serving the roulade cold, you still need to roll it before it cools completely, so roll it loosely round another sheet of paper and then unroll gently when you are ready to add the filling.

SUGGESTED FILLINGS

If serving hot, you can fill the roulade with a thick cheese sauce containing chopped ham or mushrooms or finely flaked fish. The spinach flavour goes well, too, with a filling made from bought smoked salmon paté mixed with cream cheese, though this is better with a cooler roulade. If it is too hot the filling can melt a little. Small prawns or shrimps mixed in a mayonnaise flavoured with tomato purée or a little pesto sauce also makes a nice cold starter slice.

VARIATIONS *Instead of spinach you can make the roulade with chopped and wilted salad greens or herbs – simply place them in a bowl or jug, pour boiling water over them, stir for a few seconds, then drain well. The roulade can also be made using salmon – drain a 200 g/7 oz can, mash with a fork, and add a tablespoon of cream. A filling made from finely chopped watercress mixed with cream is particularly good with this.*

OAT CUISINE | 13

My father used to describe a horse that was frisky and raring to go, as 'feeling its oats'. If oats in the diet can have this effect on a horse, what about us?

Well, there does seem to be some evidence, from research in America, that oats can be beneficial in mopping up cholesterol and adding valuable fibre. Some people have even suggested that the rise in heart disease in Scotland can be attributed to the decline in the custom of eating porridge, otherwise known as 'the poor man's filler'.

If this doesn't convince you to add some oats to your diet, perhaps the lovely nutty taste and slight crunch they give to a recipe will. Where I live, the land is more suitable to growing oats than wheat, which will only ripen further east and south, and I think the taste for oats is in-bred here. A recent appeal for the best parkin recipe in Yorkshire had me inundated with letters, and I believe I must now hold the largest collection in the country. In case you were wondering, the difference between parkin and gingerbread, which is similar, is that parkin contains oatmeal as well as flour.

Banana Oat Teabread

Makes 1 x 450 g/1 lb loaf

This cake keeps well in an airtight container for at least a week.

450 g/1 lb ripe bananas, peeled weight
2 large eggs
85 g/3 oz butter
225 g/8 oz wholemeal self-raising flour
150 g/5 oz soft brown sugar
85 g/3 oz medium oatmeal
55 g/2 oz dried banana chips

1. Preheat the oven to 180°C/350°F/Gas 4.

2. In a bowl, mash the peeled bananas with a fork. Whisk together the eggs in a separate bowl and slowly melt the butter in a small pan over a very gentle heat.

3. Measure the flour, sugar and oatmeal into a large bowl and mix together, then add the mashed banana, eggs and melted butter. Mix well until you have a fairly stiff consistency – a spoonful held above the bowl should need a shake before it drops back into the bowl. If it seems too stiff, add a tablespoon of warm water.

4. Grease and base line a 450 g/1 lb loaf tin, and spoon in the mixture, pushing it into the corners and smoothing the top. Spread the banana chips over the top, very lightly pressing them into the surface.

5. Bake for 1 hour or until a skewer inserted in the centre comes out clean. Allow to cool in the tin for 10 minutes, then take out and peel off the base paper. Leave to cool on a rack.

Flapjack

Makes 12–14 fingers

This is easy enough for older children to bake with a little supervision and makes a useful addition to a lunch box.

175 g/6 oz butter or margarine
1 tablespoon golden syrup
140 g/5 oz demerara sugar
225 g/8 oz quick porridge oats
a pinch of salt

1. Preheat the oven to 180°C/350°F/Gas 4.

2. Melt the butter or margarine, golden syrup and sugar in a pan over a very gentle heat, stirring occasionally. Add the oats and salt, mix well, and turn out into a well-greased Swiss roll tin. Smooth over the top and press into the corners with a spatula. Bake for about 30 minutes until golden brown.

3. Leave to stand in the tin for 5 minutes, then mark into squares or fingers with a knife. Allow to cool completely in the tin before taking out and breaking into pieces.

Oatcake

Serves about 10

This former staple of the British diet may well be about to make a comeback, as it is rich in cholesterol-reducing soluble dietary fibre – oats are good for you. It can be served for breakfast, like toast, with melted butter, or can be topped with cheese or jam, heated through, and eaten folded or rolled.

225 g/8 oz fine oatmeal
225 g/8 oz plain white flour
1 sachet (6 g) easy blend dried yeast
1 teaspoon salt
1 teaspoon sugar
850 ml/1½ pints warm milk and
water, combined

1. Measure the oatmeal, flour, yeast, salt and sugar into a large bowl and mix together.

2. Make a well in the centre and add the milk and water. Mix well together, either using a wooden spoon or a whisk, to make a smooth, thick batter. Leave, covered, in a warm place for 1 hour to allow the yeast to work.

3. Heat a griddle, or large, non-stick frying pan, and ladle enough batter to spread around the pan as you tip it, to the size of a plate. Cook for 2 or 3 minutes, until the surface begins to look dry and bubbles start to form. Flip over and cook for a little less time on the second side.

Moggy Parkin

Makes 9 squares

Moggy means moist and delicious, the sort of cake that improves, or 'comes again' as they used to say, with keeping in an airtight tin. This is a tea-time treat, but you could try a square of it, as we often do, as a pudding, with a helping of apple sauce.

85 g/3 oz butter or margarine
85 g/3 oz brown sugar
115 g/4 oz golden syrup or black treacle
175 g/6 oz plain flour
1½ teaspoons bicarbonate of soda
1 heaped teaspoon ground ginger
55 g/2 oz medium oatmeal
1 large egg, beaten
a little milk

1. Preheat the oven to 160°C/325°F/Gas 3 and grease and line a 20 cm/8 in cake tin.

2. Melt the butter or margarine, brown sugar and syrup in a pan over a low heat.

3. Measure the flour, bicarbonate of soda, ground ginger and oatmeal into a bowl. Mix together, then make a well in the centre. Pour in the butter and sugar mixture and beat with a wooden spoon until well combined. Add the egg and beat well until you have a thick pouring consistency – if it is too stiff, add a little milk.

4. Pour the cake mixture into the prepared cake tin and bake for about 1 hour until the centre is firm and springy to the touch. Allow to cool in the tin, then take out and cut into squares. Will keep for 2–3 weeks in an airtight container.

    NOTE *The squares can be iced and decorated with pieces of crystallized ginger if desired.*

Oat Spice Crunchies

Makes about 20

I was given this recipe by an American professor who has done a lot of research on diet, and who reckons oats are a wonder food that everyone should have more of. It's such an easy recipe for a beginner, too.

1 x 250 g/9 oz packet plain cake mix
1 teaspoon mixed spice
115 g/4 oz rolled oats
175 g/6 oz raisins
55 g/2 oz chopped nuts
55 g/2 oz wholemeal flour
3 tablespoons vegetable oil
1 medium egg, beaten
55 g/2 oz soft dark brown sugar
1 teaspoon vanilla extract
150 ml/¼ pint warm water

1. Preheat the oven to 190°C/375°F/Gas 5.

2. Measure all the ingredients into a large bowl and mix together with a wooden spoon.

3. Drop teaspoonsful of the mixture, well spaced out, on to a baking tray lined with baking parchment, and bake for 10–15 minutes until the edges are brown. You will probably need to do this in several batches. Allow the biscuits to cool a little on the baking tray, then lift them off with a fish slice or spatula on to a wire rack.

Coffee and Oat Cake

Makes 1 x 18 cm/7 in sandwich cake

55 g/2 oz porridge oats
115 g/4 oz margarine
115 g/4 oz caster sugar
85 g/3 oz self-raising flour
2 large eggs
2 heaped teaspoons instant coffee granules
2 tablespoons hot water

For the coffee cream filling
2 heaped teaspoons instant coffee granules
1 tablespoon hot water
55 g/2 oz margarine
115 g/4 oz icing sugar

To finish
55 g/2 oz porridge oats
12 walnut or pecan halves

1. First toast all the porridge oats (for both the cake and the finishing – 115 g/4 oz altogether) by placing in a dry, non-stick frying pan. Heat gently until they turn golden brown and smell nutty. You need to stir them constantly, or they will burn. Spread out the oats on a surface to cool.

2. Preheat the oven to 190°C/375°F/Gas 5. Cream the margarine and sugar in a bowl by beating them together until light and fluffy. Add a spoonful of flour and mix in.

3. Beat the eggs together in a separate bowl. Add about half to the cake mixture and mix in, then add the rest of the flour and the oats (half the amount you toasted). Mix in the rest of the eggs. Dissolve the coffee in the hot water, and mix in.

4. Divide the cake mixture between two 18 cm/7 in greased and base-lined cake tins, and smooth over the surface. Bake for 25 minutes, or until springy to the touch in the centre. Allow to cool in the tin for 5 minutes. Turn out, peel off the paper, and cool on a rack.

5. When the cakes are cool, make the coffee cream filling by dissolving the coffee in the hot water. Add the other ingredients and beat well together with a wooden spoon. Use about a third to sandwich the two cakes together. Spread another third around the sides of the cake and then, holding the cake in your hands as if rolling a wheel, roll the sides in the rest of the toasted oats so that they stick to the filling and cover the sides of the cake. Place the cake on a serving plate, and finish by spreading the last third of the filling over the top. Place the pecans or walnut halves in a circle around the edge so that each slice of cake will get a nut.

Royal Icing

This amount will cover a round cake of 20 cm/8 in diameter. A 25 cm/ 10 in square cake will need half as much again.

**2 large egg whites
2 teaspoons glycerine
750g/1 lb 10 oz icing sugar
1 tablespoon lemon juice**

If you have a hand-held electric whisk it will take a lot of the hard work out of this. Put the egg whites and glycerine in a bowl and whisk or beat together with a fork until the whites look foamy. Gradually sift in and beat together about half of the icing sugar. Beat in the lemon juice, then carry on beating in the rest of the icing sugar a bit at a time until the mixture is stiff and glossy – it should form stiff peaks. Cover the bowl with a damp cloth and leave to stand for an hour or so before spreading evenly over the cake with a palette knife. To make a smooth finish, dip the palette knife in hot water between strokes.

Butter Icing

**5 heaped tablespoons icing sugar
115g/4 oz butter, softened
1 teaspoon vanilla extract, or
1 tablespoon cocoa powder**

Beat the icing sugar a spoonful at a time into the softened butter and flavouring.

Simple Icing for Children's Fairy Cakes

For a few little buns, 6 or so, put a teaspoon of water in a small bowl and mix in a tablespoon of icing sugar – sift it if you have had the opened bag in the cupboard for a while as it may have some lumps in it. Add more icing sugar a little at a time until you get a consistency that is just stiff enough to spread.

Chocolate Fudge Icing

This makes enough to fill and cover the top and sides of a round cake that is 20–23 cm/8–9 in in diameter.

**450g/1 lb icing sugar
115g/4 oz dark chocolate
55g/2 oz butter
4 tablespoons milk**

Put all the ingredients into a heatproof bowl. Stand the bowl over a pan of barely simmering water and allow the ingredients to melt together. After a few minutes, stir together until all are melted and smooth. Take off the heat and allow to cool a little – it helps if you pour the icing into another bowl. Beat the icing with a wooden spoon as it cools and it will thicken.

You can make this in a microwave if you wish – give 30 second bursts of power and stir between each.